A CONDUCTOR'S
REPERTORY
OF
CHAMBER MUSIC

A CONDUCTOR'S REPERTORY OF CHAMBER MUSIC

Compositions for Nine to Fifteen Solo Instruments

COMPILED BY
WILLIAM SCOTT

Music Reference Collection, Number 39

GREENWOOD PRESS
Westport, Connecticut • London

Library of Congress Cataloging-in-Publication Data

Scott, William.
    A conductor's repertory of chamber music : compositions for nine
to fifteen solo instruments / compiled by William Scott.
        p.   cm.—(Music reference collection, ISSN 0736-7740 ; no.
39)
    Includes bibliographical references and index.
    ISBN 0-313-28979-4 (alk. paper)
    1. Chamber music—Bibliography.   2. Instrumental ensembles—
Bibliography.   I. Title.   II. Series.
ML128.C4S37   1993
016.785'00264—dc20   93-18458

British Library Cataloguing in Publication Data is available.

Library of Congress Catalog Card Number: 93-18458
ISBN: 0-313-28979-4
ISSN: 0736-7740

First published in 1993

Greenwood Press, 88 Post Road West, Westport, CT 06881
An imprint of Greenwood Publishing Group, Inc.

Printed in the United States of America

The paper used in this book complies with the
Permanent Paper Standard issued by the National
Information Standards Organization (Z39.48-1984).

10 9 8 7 6 5 4 3 2 1

Contents

Preface

There exists a large and diversified repertoire of chamber music written for ensembles of nine to fifteen solo players. A survey of this literature would naturally be of interest to chamber musicians and music educators as it can serve both fields as a valuable resource. Conductors, although generally not associated with chamber music, may also benefit from a study of this literature. Most universities that offer advanced degrees in orchestral conducting do not have the capacity to provide a training orchestra for the conductor. A reasonable alternative exists in the chamber ensemble which can easily be organized and requires a smaller instrumentation than an orchestra. The chamber ensemble has the potential to offer training for the developing conductor as well as to expand the repertoire of the professional conductor.

A Conductor's Repertory of Chamber Music contains over one thousand original works for chamber ensembles of nine to fifteen solo instruments. The size, volume, and manageability of an ensemble of this size, although not always requiring a conductor, encourages the employment of one. Chamber works that contain voice have been omitted as there have been several studies that cover this subject: Kay Dunlap and Barbara Winchester, *Vocal Chamber Music: A Performer's Guide*, (New York: Garland Publishing, Inc., 1985); K.S. Klaus, *Chamber Music for Solo Voice and Instruments*: 1960- 1980, (Diss. Louisiana State University and Mechanical College, 1984); and Patricia Lust, *American Vocal Chamber Music*, 1945-1989: An Annotated Bibliography, (Westport, CT: Greenwood Press, 1985). Similarly, chamber works for like groups of instruments (e.g. double bass ensembles, French horn ensembles, percussion ensembles) are not included in this study.   These works, often arrangements made to serve a pedagogical purpose, can best be considered by specialists for the instruments. The majority of works listed here are written for the mixed ensemble containing combinations of string, wind, percussion, and keyboard instruments.

   A Conductor's Repertory of Chamber Music is presented in three sections: The Repertory, the complete data base of compositions, is listed by composer and includes instrumentation, publisher, the composer's date of birth, and the number of required musicians (see *Fig. 1*). The Repertory Classified lists compositions according to similar combinations of instruments and should prove beneficial to conductors of regional orchestras who have "core" orchestras that are grouped in a similar manner. The final section is a Title Index.

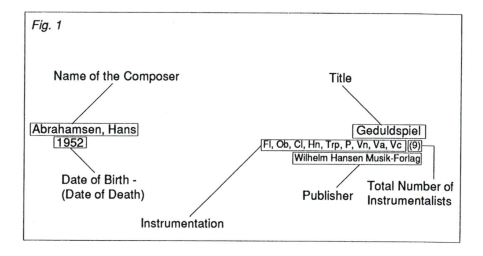

Fig. 1

Name of the Composer

Title

Abrahamsen, Hans
1952

Geduldspiel
Fl, Ob, Cl, Hn, Trp, P, Vn, Va, Vc (9)
Wilhelm Hansen Musik-Forlag

Date of Birth -
(Date of Death)

Publisher

Total Number of
Instrumentalists

Instrumentation

Acknowledgments

I have many wonderful people to thank for the completion of *A Conductor's Repertory of Chamber Music*. Dr. John Tillotson, Superintendent of Spartanburg School District No. 7, Spartanburg, South Carolina, believed in me and granted me a leave of absence to work on an advanced degree. Dr. Luise Eitel Peake, musicologist at the University of South Carolina, provided guidance and supervision for the historical aspects of this book. Darlene Fawver of Converse College served as a valuable resource for assistance in research. I am also grateful to computer specialists Paul Scott and Paul Buyer, who were so generous with their time and talent. I would like to acknowledge Olga Burtnett, Billie Edmonds, Carol Haring, Chris Helms, Anne Hicks, Meredith Mims, and William Pell for their assistance in editing. Above all, I wish to thank my parents, Russell and Apolonia Scott of Clear Lake, Wisconsin. Their lifelong commitment to the education and musical development of their children served as a continuous source of inspiration for me. Finally, this book is dedicated to my two sons, Nathan and Ryan, who were so patient in waiting for their father to finish this project.

List of Instrumental Abbreviations

Acc........................... Accordion
Acl......................Alto Clarinet
Afl ....Alto Flute
Asx ....Alto Saxophone
Ban.............................Banjo
Bcl ....Bass Clarinet
Bhn .... Bassethorn
Bn...............................Bassoon
Bsx..............Baritone Saxophone
Btrp................... Bass Trumpet
Cbn..................Contra-Bassoon
Cel..............................Celeste
Cem ....Cembalo
Cl ....Clarinet
Cor...........................Cornet
Db.......................Double Bass
Ecl .... Eb Clarinet
Egt.................... Electric Guitar
Eh......................English Horn
Eorg ....Electric Organ
Ehpd...........Electric Harpsichord
Eu.........................Euphonium
Fl...............................Flute
Fn..........................Flugelhorn
Gt .... Guitar

Har......................... Harmonica
Hn........................French Horn
Hp........................... Harp
Hpd .... Harpsichord
Hrm.......................Harmonium
Lo....................Lira Organizzata
Man.......................Mandolin
Ob.........................Oboe
Om...................Ondes Martinot
Org.........................Organ
P...............................Piano
P4h ....Piano Four Hands
Per .... Percussion
Pic ....Piccolo
Rec........................... Recorder
Ser ....Serpent
Tba........................Tuba
Trb.........................Trombone
Trp.......................... Trumpet
Tsx............... Tenor Saxophone
Va................................ Viola
Vc........................Violoncello
Vn..............................Violin
Zit..........................Zither

Instruments separated by a diagonal line are performed by one player
(e.g. Fl/Pic, Cl/Bcl).

List of Music Publishers

Ahn & Simrock..Wiesbaden, Germany
Albert J. Kunzelmann ....Schott
Aldo Bruzzichelli...Margun Music
Alexander Broude, Inc...................................... New York, New York
Alphonse Leduc .... Paris, France
Editorial Alpuerto...Madrid, Spain
American Composers Alliance................................... New York, New York
American Music Center.. New York, New York
Andraund .... Southern Music
Ars Polona.. Warsaw, Poland
Artia...Prague, Czechoslovakia
Artisan Music Press...West Nyack, New York
Associated Music Publishers .... New York, New York
Autograph Editions..West Nyack, New York
S. Eugene Bailey.. Northfield, Minnesota
Bärenreiter & Neuwerk ....Kassel-Wilhelmshöhe, Germany
Bärenreiter Verlag...Kassel-Wilhelmshöhe, Germany
Baxter-Northrup ....Friendship, New York
M.P. Belaieff... Frankfurt, Germany
Belwin-Mills Company ....Melville, New York
M.P. Belaieff... Frankfurt, Germany
Billaudot Editions Musicales .... Paris, France
BMI Canada Ltd....................................American Music Publishers
Boelke-Bomart Pub... Hillsdale, New York
Bossey & Hawkes ....Oceanside, New York
Boston Music Co.. Boston, Massachusetts
Bote & Bock ....Berlin, Germany
Branch.. West Babylon, New York
Breitkopf & Härtel..Leipzig, Germany
Broude Brothers, Ltd .... New York, New York

Aldo Bruzzichelli..Newton Centre, Massachusetts
Editio Musica Budapest ....Budapest, Hungary
C.F. Vieweg Musikverlag....................................Berlin, Germany
Cambridge Music Shop....................................Cambridge, England
Canadian Music Centre...................................... Ontario, Canada
Carisch S.P.A ....Milan, Italy
Carl Fischer .... New York, New York
Casa Musicale Sonzogno......................................Milan, Italy
CeBeDem .... Brussels, Belgium
Centre Belge de Documentation Musicale.......................... Brussels, Belgium
Ceský Hudební Fond.................................Prague, Czechoslovakia
Chappel & Co., Inc... Paris, France
J.W. Chester Music Ltd.......................................London, England
M.M. Cole Publishing Co..................................Chicago, Illinois
Composer's Autograph Publications .... Hamilton, Ohio
Composer/Performer Edition ....Sacramento, California
Composers' Facsimile Edition .... New York, New York
Cor Publishing Co.. Massapequa, New York
Costallat...Billaudot
Crescendo Music Sales Co.....................................Dallas, Texas
Curwen ....London, England
VEB Deutscher Verlag ....Leipzig, Germany
Donemus... Amsterdam, Holland
Edicije Društva Slovenskih ....Ljubljana, Yugoslavia
DSS Editions ....Belgrade, Yugoslavia
Dunvagen Music Pub. Inc.................................... New York, New York
Durand & Cie... Paris, France
E.C. Kerby, Ltd... Ontario, Canada
Edward B. Marks Music Corp..................................... New York, New York
Edwin F. Kalmus...Boca Raton, Florida
Elkan-Vogel..Bryn Mawr, Pennsylvania
Ensemble Publications... Buffalo, New York
Rudolph Erdmann Musik-Verlag ....Wiesbaden, Germany
Robert Erickson..Berkeley, California
Editorial de Musica Española Contemporanea ....Madrid, Spain
Eulenberg .... Adliswil-Zürich, Switzerland
Edition Eulenberg...Peters
European American Music ....Totowa, New Jersey
F.E.C. Leuckart Verlag .... Munich, Germany
Faber Music Ltd...London, England
Feedback-Studio-Verlag .... Cologne, Germany
Fétis.. Brussels, Belgium
Finnish Music Information Centre............................. Helsinki, Finland
Fleischer..Philadelphia, Pennsylvania
Franco Colombo, Inc.. Belwin
Samuel French, Inc.. New York, New York

G. Schirmer .... New York, New York
Geiringer ....Vienna, Austria
General Music Publishing Co.................................. Boston, Massachusetts
Gustav Bosse Verlag...Regensburg, Germany
Hans Gerig Musikverlag..Breitkopf & Härtel
Heinrichshofen Verlag.. Wilhelmshaven, Germany
Henri Lemoine & Cie .... Paris, France
Hermann Moeck Verlag...Celle, Germany
Heugel & Cie.. Paris, France
Highgate Press.. New York, New York
Hofmeister Musikverlag ....Leipzig, Germany
Hug & Company ....Zürich, Switzerland
International Music Company...................................... New York, New York
Islenzk ....Elkan-Vogel
Israeli Music Institute ....Tel Aviv, Israel
Israeli Music Pub., Ltd...Tel Aviv, Israel
James Abersold...New Albany, Indiana
Jobert & Cie .... Paris, France
Joseph Boonin, Inc.. European American Music
Joshua Corp...General Music Publishing Co.
June Emerson-Wind Music.. York, England
Junne.. Munich, Germany
Kahnt..Peters
Kendor Music, Inc.. Delevan, New York
Robert King Music Co......................................North Easton, Massachusetts
Leeds .... Belwin
Lienau..Berlin, Germany
H. Litolff's Verlag.. Frankfurt, Germany
Lorenzi.. Dayton, Ohio
Luck's Music Library.. Madison Heights, Michigan
Ludwig Doblinger ....Vienna, Austria
Harold Lyche..Oslo, Norway
Mannheimer Musik-Verlag.. Mannheim, Germany
Manuscript Curtis Institute ....Philadelphia, Pennsylvania
Manuscript Publications...................................... Wrightsville, Pennsylvania
Margun Music, Inc...Newton Centre, Massachusetts
MCA Music..Belwin-Mills
McGinnis & Marx.. New York, New York
Mentor Music, Inc..Brookfield, Connecticut
Merion Music... Theodore Presser
Mezhdunarodhaya Kniga .... G. Schirmer
Mills ....Melville, New York
MJQ Music Inc.. New York, New York
Edition Modern.. Munich, Germany
Edition Moeck...Celle, Germany
Willy Müller-Süddeutscher Musikverlag ....Heidelberg, Germany

Murdoch..London, England
Edition Musicus, Inc...............................Stamford, Connecticut
Musica Rara...Monteux, France
Musica Viva...Sussex, England
Musical Evergreen...............................West Nyack, New York
Musiikin Tiedotuskeskus.............................Helsinki, Finland
Muziekuitgaven Metropolis.........................Antwerp, Belgium
Nordiska Musikforlaget.............................Stockholm, Sweden
Novello & Co., Ltd....................................Kent, England
Verlag Neue Musik....................................Berlin, Germany
Ongaku Notomo Sha Corp..............................Tokyo, Japan
Opus Music Publishers..............................Chicago, Illinois
Oxford University Press............................London, England
Panton...Prague, Czechoslovakia
Peer International.............................Southern Music Pub. Co.
C.F. Peters Corp.................................New York, New York
Pohl...Basel, Switzerland
Polskie Wydawnictwo Muzyczne......................Warsaw, Poland
Pro Musica Verlag....................................Leipzig, Germany
Rahter.......................................Associated Music Publishers
Richault...Paris, France
G. Ricordi & Co....................................Milan, Italy
Ries & Erler...Berlin, Germany
Rongwen Music, Inc................................Broude Brothers, Ltd.
Sadlova Edice.....................................Prague, Czechoslovakia
Editions Salabert...................................Paris, France
Sansone..Peer-Southern
Scherzando...Brussels, Belgium
Schmid...Leipzig, Germany
Schott...Brussels, Belgium
Schott & Company, Ltd............................London, England
B. Schotts' Söhne..................................Mainz, Germany
Schuberth Verlag....................................Leipzig, Germany
Seesaw Music Corp..................................New York, New York
Senart...Paris, France
Sesac, Incorporated................................New York, New York
Shawnee Press, Inc.............Delaware Water Gap, Pennsylvania
Sieber...Costallat
N. Simrock...Hamburg, Germany
Sirius-Verlag.......................................Berlin, Germany
Slovensky Hudobny Fond.......................Bratislava, Czechoslovakia
Smith Publications.................................Baltimore, Maryland
The Society for Publishing Danish Music...............Copenhagen, Denmark
Southern Music Co.................................San Antonio, Texas
Southern Music Pub. Co., Inc......................New York, New York
Spratt...Ft. Lauderdale, Florida

Introduction:
A Historical Survey of
Conducting Chamber Music

Chamber music refers to music which is written for an ensemble of solo performers. An important aspect of chamber music is the interplay of parts - salient features being the give and take among equal partners, and interpretation by agreement of each member of the ensemble. The majority of chamberworks: string trios, string quartets, piano trios, woodwind quartets, brass quintets, woodwind quintets, etc., does not need a conductor. Musicians are required to spend an adequate amount of time in preparation of the complete score as well as their own individual parts. When not needed, a conductor would most likely detract from the interplay of the ensemble members and take away from the effectiveness of the performance.

The size of a chamber ensemble is often the determinant as to whether a conductor is needed. It can be difficult for more than eight players to remain in good ensemble without a conductor. The distance between the end musicians coupled with the large tonal volume that can be produced with larger ensembles can make hearing very difficult. The personalities and musical responses of more than eight musicians can make compromise among the players a difficult goal to attain.[1] Certainly a work like the Richard Strauss *Metamorphosen* for 23 solo strings, although in the chamber style with one player to a part, requires the assistance of a conductor for a convincing performance.

The difficulty of a chamber work can also mandate the use of a conductor. In 1912, the first performance of Arnold Schoenberg's

Pierrot Lunaire, a work for vocal soloist and an ensemble of five instrumentalists, was conducted by the composer. Another example of a small ensemble requiring a conductor is Béla Bartók's *Sonata for Two Pianos and Percussion.* The work was first performed with Bartók and his wife as pianists with Hermann Scherchen conducting. Although often performed without a conductor, the rhythmic difficulty of the work would certainly favor the collaboration of a conductor.

In discussing conducted and non-conducted performances of Schoenberg's *Quintet,* Opus 26, Robert Craft indicates that the most convincing performance of this difficult chamber work is given with a conductor. An ensemble can be assisted in the following ways: the conductor, being in a position to hear the entire ensemble, is helpful in the matter of dynamic balance; the conductor can indicate the connections and the dovetailings of the phrases; and in works in which voice leading jumps around with great rapidity, the conductor is able to assist the performers and listeners to follow the musical line and to realize the form of the composition.[2]

The role of the conductor, whether it be to conduct a large post-Romantic orchestra or a quartet of players, is to assist the performers in making music. The quality of players, the difficulty of the music, and the amount of rehearsal time are factors which need to be considered when determining whether a conductor should be employed. Therefore, the purpose of this book is not to recommend which chamber works should or should not be conducted, but to survey the large body of music that exists with the limited instrumentation of nine to fifteen solo instruments, which can be considered a conductor's repertory of chamber music. Music written for ensembles with a featured soloist or with singers is excluded from this study, because the interplay of equal or nearly equally important musical parts is considered a necessary ingredient of chamber music.

During the Baroque era and up to the late eighteenth century, *Musica da Camera* had a different meaning. At that time music was divided into categories based on its function in the church, theater, and at home. Chamber music referred to all music played in the home, including both instrumental and vocal media, in solo, ensemble, or orchestral settings.[3]

One of the Baroque forms of instrumental chamber music is the trio sonata, which is characterized by two treble instruments and bass. In some trio sonatas the bass serves a melodic function, as in a fugal movement of a *Sonata da Chiesa*. In others the bass has a more subordinate role, serving mainly a harmonic function.[4] Trio sonatas first appeared in print in 1607, and as early as 1693 were referred to as *Divertimentos*.[5] Depending upon the location of the performance and the function of the music, trio sonatas could either be performed by small or large ensembles. When performed "da camera" they were usually done with one instrument to a part; in a church setting, "da chiesa," where volume was needed, they were played orchestrally with several players for each line. Sulzer, in his *Allgemeine Theorie der schönen Künste*, tells us about this practice:

> There are trios which are set in the learned and strict church style containing well-shaped fugues. They generally consist of two violin parts and a bass part, and are even called church trios. These must be set with more than one instrument to a part: otherwise they have no power. The strict fugue which, on solemn occasions and in strongly set musical performances, moves all people by the sonority, solemnity and uniformity of its progression, has no appeal for the amateur of feeling in a chamber trio where each part is set only singly. It is only appealing to the connoisseur, for whom art in any form is welcome.[6]

A similar practice can be observed in the performance of the concerto grosso, a multi-movement composition in which a small group of soloists, the concertino, is contrasted with a larger instrumental ensemble, the ripieno. The first concerti grossi were trio sonatas to which ripieno parts were added, for instance, Corelli's *Concerti Grossi con Duoi Violini, e Violoncello di Concertino Obbligati e Duoi altri Violini, Viola, e Basso ad Arbitrio che se Potranno Radoppiare* ("Concerti Grossi with two Violins and Cello of the Obbligato Concertino and two other Violins, Viola, and the Bass which can be Arbitrarily Doubled"). Since the soloists also joined in the tutti, these concertos could be played by as few as seven performers, one to a part in *da camera* style, or with a tutti orchestra of twenty or more players in *da chiesa* style.[7]

Publications of instrumental ensemble music in the Baroque period did not specify whether solo or orchestral performance was preferred, a tradition that was carried on through the early Classical period. The task of determining whether one or more players should be apportioned to each melody part was usually left to the players. An exception was the thorough bass which was normally doubled (keyboard with cello or bass) or tripled (cello, bass, and keyboard).

The disappearance of the basso continuo during the eighteenth century marks the transition from Baroque to Classical chamber music. Classical chamber music stresses the interplay of all solo parts, each having a value of independence. The Baroque thorough bass, while conveniently filling in the harmonies, negates this independence of the parts by doubling the bass line and often doubling some of the inner voices as well. Without thorough bass the texture of two melody instruments and one bass without keyboard often would sound incomplete. To make their harmonies more complete, composers added a fourth voice, the viola, and in some cases a couple of horns, to the former trio sonata. The earliest works to use trio sonata instrumentation with viola were divertimentos and symphonies.[8]

Divertimento was a catch-all term used throughout the eighteenth century. It is the title of choice in the repertory of Classical chamber music, appearing more often than any other designation and including the greatest variety of scorings and styles.[9] The term "divertimento" does not designate a genre, but was merely a title for non-orchestral instrumental music which could be considered analogous to the modern term "composition." The early divertimentos could be duets, trios, quartets, quintets, or larger groups and included both serious and light music. The three main types of instrumentation used in the early Classical divertimento are: 1) keyboard, usually with accompanying instruments; 2) wind ensembles, and 3) strings which are often augmented by winds.[10] These last two categories include compositions for larger ensembles of instruments and therefore could require the assistance of a conductor.

During the 1780s the term "Divertimento" became consistently associated with light entertainment music, composed exclusively for solo instruments and considered as an amusement for both listener and performer.[11] It generally comprises one to nine movements (but may contain as many as thirteen), and it is simliar to the Baroque suite and *Sonata da Camera* with the inclusion of dance movements.[12]

Other titles often used to designate entertainment music are *Harmoniemusik, Tafelmusik, Serenade, Cassation,* and *Notturno.* All fall under the category of *Divertimento,* "amusement," and could be used interchangeably. They differ only in the time of day and type of function for which they were intended.

Harmoniemusik, refers to wind band music of the eighteenth century, composed for an ensemble of four to fourteen musicians. It was intended to serve as background music for both indoor and outdoor social functions, and a special role of the musicians was to provide entertainment during and after meals. The term *Tafelmusik* can therefore be used interchangeably with *Harmoniemusik.*[13] *Serenades* were orginally meant to be performed in the evening by a lover at his lady's window, or to serve as a greeting or to honor an important person.[14] The term "serenade" was often given to a movement of a composition with pizzicato accompaniment that would suggest the guitar or mandolin.[15] *Cassations,* also performed in the open air, differ from serenades in that they were not restricted to evening hours.[16]The term *Notturno* designates outdoor music which was played late at night, generally around eleven o'clock.[17]

This outdoor literature necessitated the exclusion of the basso continuo from the ensemble, and this was to become the major difference between Baroque and Classical chamber music.[18] Musicians would often play for one dignitary and then walk off and perform elsewhere, which naturally discouraged the use of the harpsichord.[19] In a similar fashion, the cello was not used as a bass part for outdoor music because of the inconvenience of having to use a chair.[20]

In Mozart's day there were two types of serenades, orchestral and for solo players. The full orchestra serenade is designed for grand celebrations, such as the wedding of a rich or famous person (*Haffner Serenade*), the end of a university year, or the Archbishop's name day. The other type of serenade is less formal, intended to be performed by solo players for a more modest occasion.[21]The instrumentation of a serenade will often give us a clue as to the intended performance practice. In Mozart's Serenades K. 185, 203, 204, and 250 (the *Haffner*) one or more movements are set in the *Symphonie Concertante* style. This implies orchestral performance, because a solo violin is needed in addition to the first and second violin parts.

Works of a more serious nature - symphonies, concertos, and *Symphonie Concertantes* - could also be performed as chamber music. Early quartets of Haydn and Boccherini were published under the title of "Symphonie" or "Sinfonia."[22] Some of the early symphonies designate solo strings in the manuscript, for example Ignaz Pleyel's *Periodical Symphonies* which are scored in the following manner: 2 Oboi, 2 Corni, Violino 1, Violino 2, Viola, Cello, and Basso.[23] "Violino" is singular and means "violin." If performed with single players to a part, these symphonies could be considered nonets. Concertos also had the option of being performed in chamber music settings.[24] The title page of the violin concertos of Maddalena Laura Lombardini Sirmen reads "Six Concertos in Nine Parts ...." The score incorporates the singular term "violino," also suggesting a chamber performance.[25]

The *Sinfonia Concertante* was a hybrid musical form that contained elements of both symphony and concerto. It became very popular in Paris in the 1770s and flourished until about 1830. Basically a concerto for more than one solo instrument (generally between two and seven), it was light-hearted in nature and similar to the *Divertimento*.[26] The instrumentation of the accompanying orchestra generally paralleled that of the symphony of the time, thus either for chamber ensemble or orchestra.[27]

"Divertimento" dies out as a title after 1800. Although seldom found, it appears again in the twentieth century when composers use the term as it existed at the end of the eighteenth century. Examples are Stravinsky's Divertimento from *Le Baiser de la Fée* and Bartók's *Divertimento for Strings*. This music is light in character, and its purpose is to entertain.

The orchestra in the middle eighteenth century was basically an eight-part ensemble, two violins, viola, bass (which included cello and bass) and two pairs of winds (oboes and horns). These ensembles could be considered string quartets with added obbligato parts for wind instruments. The winds ordinarily performed one of three roles: they played chords to provide a harmonic backdrop to the strings, they doubled the melody in the violins, or they performed short solo passages. Toward the end of the eighteenth century, one finds in Mozart's and Haydn's symphonies the addition of clarinets, trumpets, and flutes. The general trend in orchestration was toward a greater independence of winds and strings, either alone or in new combinations. Another trend includes the separation of the cello and bass which results in a five-part string texture.[28] The average size of the eighteenth century court orchestra was between five and twenty-five players; although a few, like the orchestra at Mannheim, were larger.[29]

The nineteenth century witnessed major sociological changes that had a great influence on music. The industrial revolution coupled with the rise of the middle class helped to promote the emergence of the public concert, changes in the functions of music, and new aesthetic ideals. With the movement toward military and political consolidation, many of the smaller court orchestras were discontinued.[30]

The middle classes and their new keen interest in music changed the Baroque and early eighteenth-century ideal of private music making in the courts to public concerts in large halls or theaters. This new music, however, was devoid of function. It was not used for dance or march, to accompany religious or court ritual, or to serve as background music for ceremony or dinner. The conversion from private to public performance before a paying audience made it a financial necessity for the composers to respond to the tastes of the growing public.[31]Sacred and secular vocal solos, formerly associated with the church and opera house, were often eliminated from public concert programs and replaced by larger orchestral works.[32] The genres which were most often used to communicate with the mass public were symphony, overture, concerto, and symphonic poem.[33]

The Romantic ideal of the sublime also contributed to the increasing size of the orchestras, concert halls, and compositions. Defined by Aubin Louis Millin, in his *Dictionnaire des beaux-arts* (1806) and by Gustav Schilling, in his *Universal-Lexikon der Tonkunst* (1835-1838): "For something to be sublime it must be on a large scale: large in itself, in its power or in its extent or shape."[34] Thus, Romantic composers were encouraged to express the "highest perfection of Art" with the grandest possible artistic gesture. Orchestral, operatic, and liturgical forms grew to such proportions that they necessitated massive orchestras.[35]

The instrumentation of Wagner's earliest operas, *Die Feen* (1834) and *Das Liebesverbot* (1836), for instance, resembles that of the Classical orchestra, written for strings with winds in pairs. For *Tannhäuser* (1845), he still uses winds in pairs but expands the brass section to four horns, three trumpets, three trombones, and one tuba. The woodwinds are expanded to groups of three in *Lohengrin* (1850) and *Tristan und Isolde* (1865). In *Der Ring des Nibelungen*, (completed in 1874), Wagner employs quadruple woodwind scoring and expands the brass section to eight French horns and quadruple trumpets and trombones. This Romantic desire for "largesse" was continued by composers into the twentieth century. Gustav Mahler uses quintuple woodwind scoring in his Sixth Symphony (1906), and Richard Strauss adds a quartet of saxophones in *Symphonia Domestica* (1904). Arnold Schoenberg takes it one step further by exceeding quintuple woodwind scoring in his *Gurrelieder* (1903). This work calls for a section of 25 woodwinds, which alone is larger than the size of Haydn's entire 1783 orchestra at Esterház.[36]

All of these factors, the Romantic ideal of sublimity, the increase in the size of the orchestra, the emergence of the public concert series, as well as the rising middle class and the general decline of the aristocracy, contributed to the popularity of the large orchestral forms and somewhat stifled the growth of chamber music in the nineteenth century. Nevertheless, the medium of the smaller chamber ensemble, the string quartet or piano trio, continued to remain popular with major composers.

The nineteenth-century style of composition for large chamber ensembles was largely influenced by Beethoven's *Septet*, Op. 20. The *Septet* was premiered on the same program with Beethoven's First Symphony in 1800. The work resembles the eighteenth-century divertimentos of Haydn and Mozart with a six-movement scheme. The wind instruments, however, are treated as integral parts of the structure, not as accompanying instruments. It is the first work for a mixed instrumental group in which winds are given equal treatment as the strings, beginning a trend that becomes evident in works for the large chamber ensemble throughout the nineteenth century.[37]

The Schubert *Octet* was commissioned by Count Ferdinand von Troyer, a clarinetist who requested an old-style *Divertimento* similar to Beethoven's work.[38] Schubert's instrumentation for the *Octet* is the same as that of the Beethoven *Septet* (violin, viola, cello, double bass, clarinet, bassoon, and horn) with the addition of a second violin part. There are several other similarities. In both compositions we find a six-movement scheme; an eighteen-measure *Adagio* introduction to the *Allegro* first movement; second movements which are *Adagio* in tempo and begin with clarinet solos; a theme-and-variation movement sandwiched between two dance movements; and finales which begin with a slower introduction. The *Octet*, one of Schubert's few works for large chamber ensemble, was written 24 years later than Beethoven's *Septet*. It typifies the early Romantic desire for largeness being approximately twice as long as the Beethoven model.

Very few chamber works from this period exist for groups of nine to fifteen instruments. What literature we have can be categorized into three groups: four-movement works modeled after the symphony, works composed for special occasions, and functional music of various kinds.

Nonets by Charles Gounod (*Petite Symphonie*, for Nine Winds), Josef Rheinberger, Louise Farrenc, and Ludwig Spohr are similar to early nineteenth-century symphonies. We find the four-movement scheme which includes sonata forms, a dance movement, and a slow movement. A further similarity to the symphony is that nonets are about equally long in duration. The most prolific composer of nineteenth-century *Nonetts* and *Dezetts* is Heinrich Molbe (whose real name is Henrich Freiherr von Bach). His six nonets and twelve dezetts account for almost half of the chamber music written for large groups during this period.

Two prominent composers who wrote chamber works for large groups of instruments are Richard Strauss and Antonin Dvořák. Strauss' first work for such an ensemble, the *Serenade for Winds*, Opus 7, is a one-movement work in modified sonata form scored for two flutes, two oboes, two clarinets, four French horns, two bassoons, and contrabassoon. This Serenade proved so successful that Strauss was asked by the eminent conductor Hans von Bülow to write a four-movement work using the same instrumentation. The result was *Suite Op. 4* which von Bülow adopted into the repertory of the *Meiningen Hofkapelle*.[39] Dvořák's *Serenade in D Minor* can also be conceived as a symphony for solo instruments. It is scored for two oboes, two clarinets, two bassoons, three French horns, cello, bass, and contrabassoon (ad lib.).

Two works that come to mind as having been written for special occasions are the *Siegfried Idyll* and *Le Carnaval des Animaux*. Richard Wagner's *Siegfried Idyll* represents his only work in the chamber music idiom. This *Pièce d'Occasion* was presented in 1870 as a birthday present to his wife Cosima, with fifteen musicians performing under Wagner's direction. The work was dubbed *Treppenmusik* ("staircase music") because the first performance was played on the staircase of Villa Triebschen. The *Idyll* is a one-movement fantasy which is composed in the form of an arch (ABCBA). Saint-Saëns wrote *Le Carnaval des Animaux* in 1886, as a surprise for a private concert on Shrove Tuesday. The work is scored for eleven solo instruments and consists of fourteen short movements, musical caricatures that include quotations from Offenbach, Berlioz, Mendelssohn, and his own *Danse Macabre*. Very few performances of the work took place during his lifetime as Saint-Saëns allowed the publication of the *Carnaval* only after his death.

While the functional role of chamber music in the eighteenth century diminished in the nineteenth, there are a few Romantic works that can be categorized as functional music. Carl Maria von Weber wrote a composition for ten trumpets and percussion titled *Marcia Vivace*. The piece is a cavalry tune written in 1822 for the Corps of Trumpeters of the Prussian king's own regiment, the *Schwarze Husaren* (the "Black Hussars"). The melody of this march also occurs in Weber's opera *Euryanthe*.[40] Franz Schubert's *Eine kleine Trauermusik* ("A Little Funeral Music") of 1813 is a very short work, and like the Weber march was composed for a specific function. It is scored for a nonet of winds and French horns.

The blossoming of the symphony orchestra and its literature in the nineteenth century naturally dwarfed the importance of chamber music. In the twentieth century the Romantic sound ideal was abandoned and preference shifted toward clarity of line. This anti-Romantic trend was to give rebirth to the value and function of the chamber ensemble.

The linear conception of music embraced by many early twentieth-century composers was difficult to express with the large orchestra. Schoenberg preferred the chamber-sized orchestra because it best conveyed economy, clarity, and precision. He writes in *Interview mit mir Selbst* (1928):

> My goal has been for sometime to find for my orchestral structures a form such that the fullness and saturation of sound shall be obtained only through the use of relatively few voices.[41]

Although earlier works, like his *Gurrelieder* of 1903, employ a massive orchestra, Schoenberg shows his preference for the chamber ensemble with two works written in 1907; the *Chamber Symphony* (scored for fifteen soloists) and *Pierrot Lunaire* (scored for six musicians).

The musical sophistication of some audiences also helped to encourage composers to favor the chamber ensemble. Schoenberg speaks rather disparagingly of the fondness for the monumental in America:

> If it were not for America, we in Europe would be composing only for reduced orchestras, chamber orchestras. But in countries with younger cultures, less refined nerves require the monumental: when the sense of hearing is incapable of compelling the imagination, one must add the sense of sight.[42]

The interest of composers in past styles of the Baroque and Classical periods also encouraged music for the reduced orchestra and chamber ensemble. The Stravinsky *Octet*, scored for eight winds, is reminiscent of the wind *partitas* of Rosetti. The three-movement work mirrors late eighteenth century works in the symmetry of its structure. The first movement has similarities to sonata form, the slow movement is a theme with variations, and the third is a rondo. In a similar way, sonorities of Bach's

Brandenburg Concertos and orchestral suites are evident in many neo-Classical and Baroque-revival works of the 1920s and 30s. The "back to Bach" trend is especially evident in Stravinsky's *Dumbarton Oaks Concerto* which has several features resembling the Baroque concerto grosso in both scoring and the treatment of solo groups. Other chamber works which demonstrate traits from earlier periods include Hindemith's *Kammermusik* and Martinů's *Tre Ricercari* and *Concerto Grosso*.[43]

Economic conditions certainly influenced the popularity of the chamber ensemble in the 20th century. This is most clearly exemplified by Stravinsky when he describes *L'Histoire du Soldat*:

> The shoe-string economics of the original *L'Histoire* production kept me to a handful of instruments, but this confinement did not act as a limitation, as my musical ideas were already directed toward a solo-instrumental style.[44]

The result was a work that required a limited company of players and a small pickup band of clarinet, bassoon, trumpet, trombone, violin, double bass, and percussion. The Society for Private Musical Performances, founded by Schoenberg in 1918 for the express purpose of performing new compositions, was similarly guided by the lack of financial resources. Although works of all kinds were premiered by this organization, it was unable to afford a large orchestra, and many works were arranged for a chamber music instrumentation. Thus, composers who wanted to have their works performed were encouraged to write for this smaller medium.[45]

Commissioned compositions, another financial consideration, also affected the movement toward smaller media. Winnaretta Singer, daughter of the sewing machine magnate Isaac Singer, commissioned several works for chamber ensemble in Paris after World War I: Igor Stravinsky's *Renard* (1922); Eric Satie's *Socrate* (1920); and Manuel de Falla's *El retablo de maese Pedro* (1923). Other Singer commissions include chamber works by Germaine Tailleferre, Jean Wiener, Karol Szymanowski, Darius Milhaud, Francis Poulenc, Nicolas Nabokov, Kurt Weill, and Jean Françaix. In her memoirs, she gives us an insight to the anti-Romantic, anti-Wagnerian ideal which was prevalent during the early 1900s and her preference for the smaller orchestra:

> I had the impression that, after Richard Wagner and Richard Strauss, the days of big orchestras were over and that it would be delightful to return to a small orchestra of well chosen players and instruments.[46]

In the United States, Elizabeth Sprague Coolidge favored the performance of chamber music. She donated an auditorium to the Library of Congress and commissioned works to be performed there. Among her commissions is the Copland ballet *Appalachian Spring*, originally scored for thirteen instruments. Orchestras as well as music associations were also patrons of chamber works. The Basel Chamber Orchestra and *Collegium Musicum* of Zürich both fostered the promotion of the chamber ensemble with approximately one hundred commissioned works for small orchestra.[47]

Jazz and popular music also played an important role in the development of the twentieth-century chamber ensemble. As Stravinsky says:

> The *Histoire* ensemble resembles the jazz band in that each instrumental category - strings, woodwinds, brass, and percussion - is represented by both treble and bass components. The instruments themselves are jazz legitimates, too, except the bassoon, which is my substitution for the saxophone.... Jazz meant, in any case, a wholly new sound in my music, and *Histoire* marks my final break with the Russian orchestral school.[48]

Several other European composers modeled their works after the American jazz band. Milhaud's *La Création du Monde*, for instance, is set for a chamber-sized orchestra which includes the saxophone and an enlarged complement of percussion. The use of "blue notes" also evokes its affinity with the American jazz band.[49] Music that accompanied variety shows represented *Kleinkunst*, popular art, which twentieth-century composers used to supplant their nineteenth-century ideal of high romantic art. Schoenberg's *Nachtwandler* is such a work. The instrumentation, text, and style of this work parody the music of the German cabaret.

The literature for the chamber ensemble increased dramatically as the United States developed into an important center for the musical avant-garde. Charles Ives wrote over 25 works for chamber orchestra between 1900 and 1917, some with the inclusion of voices. Ives considered these to be experimental in nature and describes their purpose in his *Memos*:

> Some of these shorter pieces like these (for a few players, and called chamber music pieces) were in part made to strengthen the ear muscles, the mind muscles and perhaps the Soul muscles too.... I gave the ears plenty of new sound experiences.[50]

Edgard Varèse, Henry Cowell, John Cage, and their successors were to use the small chamber orchestra for their "experiments" in sound and texture.[51] The Pan-American Association and the International Composers Guild, two organizations which promoted avant-garde music in the United States, sponsored concerts of contemporary music in New York, and their policy was to program only works for the small ensemble. Many chamber works by Carl Ruggles, Charles Ives, Adolph Weiss, Wallingford Riegger, Edgard Varèse, and Henry Cowell received their first performances in this way.[52]

In general, the twentieth-century chamber ensemble echoes the symphonic trend towards the increased prominence of percussion instruments and the equal partnership of the woodwinds, brass, and strings as the foundation of the orchestra.[53] Novel combinations of instruments now seem to be the rule rather than the exception, and the twentieth-century sound ideal is "percussive."

This change in the role of instruments was certainly affected by their development, which for winds, brass, and percussion, came much later than for the strings. An important factor contributing to the shift from the string-dominated ensembles of the eighteenth and nineteenth centuries to the ideal of equal partnership can be attributed to the popularity of band programs in America.

At the turn of the century, many states passed "band laws" which levied special taxes on the community to support free band concerts.[54] Band participation also became commonplace during sporting events. These trends coupled with renewed interest in the military band during the First World War helped to promote the practice of band music in the public schools of the United States. This new market attracted such major composers as Hindemith and Stravinsky who wrote for the band, the wind ensemble, and the wind-dominated chamber ensemble.

Many of the wind ensemble works by major composers, such as Bernstein's *Pennsylvania Overture*; Hovhaness' *Symphony No. 4*; Krenek's *Symphony for Winds and Percussion*, Op. 34; and Stravinsky's *Symphony of Wind Instruments*; are written for more than fifteen solo instruments, (therefore not included in this study). The most prominent wind-dominated works for chamber ensembles of nine to fifteen instruments are: Paul Hindemth's *Konzertmusik*, Op. 49; Francis Poulenc's *Suite Française*, Ned Rorem's *Sinfonia for Fifteen Wind Instruments*, and Edgard Varèse's *Hyperprism* and *Intégrales*. Vaughan Williams' *Scherzo alla Marcia*, one of four movements from his Eighth Symphony, is scored for fifteen wind instruments. Wind-dominated works naturally include fanfares which are often scored for large brass choirs with percussion. Examples of these are Copland's *Fanfare for a Common Man*, and Joan Tower's *Second* and *Third Fanfare for the Uncommon Woman*.

The role of percussion instruments has radically changed from the eighteenth century to the present. During the Classical period, only a pair of timpani was considered to be a basic accessory of the orchestra. Now percussion instruments share an equal status with the other members of the orchestral family.[55] We now have a large body of percussion ensemble music which is most often performed with a conductor. One of the most famous works in this genre is George Antheil's *Ballet Méchanique*. The work is scored for six percussionists and four pianos, and the pianos are conceived not as melodic instruments, but as additions to the percussion battery, playing tone clusters. Other major composers who contributed to this medium are: Carlos Chávez, *Toccata for Percussion Instruments*; Alan Hovhanness, *October Mountain*; Ronald LoPresti, *Sketch for Percussion*; and Edgard Varèse, *Ionisation*.

The growing interest in non-Western music cultures helped to promote percussion instruments. The Javanese *Gamelan* at the Paris Universal Exposition of 1889 fascinated Debussy and other composers, suggesting a new type of instrumentation - an orchestra dominated by percussion instruments. The "gamelan" may vary in size from just a few instruments to over 75, the main melody instruments being idiophones such as xylophones and gongs.[56] Canadian-American composer Colin McPhee, for instance, transcribed Balinese music for Western instruments and also founded several gamelan ensembles in the United States.

The interest in exotic percussive sounds promoted the development of new instruments. Harry Partch invented a large number of idiophones made of wood (Quadrangularis Reversum), bamboo (Boos I and II), glass (Cloud-Chamber Bowls), and metal (Gourd Tree). His tuning systems, however, make it impossible for these instruments to be used in any other context.[57] Composers also used non-musical items as percussion instruments. Two different sizes of airplane propellers and electric door bells are used for George Antheil's *Ballet Méchanique*, and Varèse introduced typewriters, sirens, and other appliances in his scores.

The equal partnership of the percussion instruments with other solo instruments and even the human voice is evident in *Le Marteau sans Maître*, by Pierre Boulez. This is a chamber work for alto voice and six instruments: flute, violin, guitar, and percussions. Three percussionists play the xylophone and vibraphone as well as side drum, bongos, maracas, double cowbell, tam-tam, gong, cymbal, two cymbalettes, and triangle.[58] *Xochipilli - An Imagined Aztec Music*, by Carlos Chávez, scored for piccolo, flute, Eb clarinet, trombone, and six percussions, also can be called a percussion-dominated ensemble.

Large string-dominated ensembles are not as prevalent now as they were in the eighteenth and nineteenth centuries. The string nonets composed by Aaron Copland and David Diamond are probably the best known. Both are scored for three violins, three violas, and three cellos, the same instrumentation as J. S. Bach's *Brandenburg Concerto No. 3* minus the continuo. Another link with the Baroque model is Copland's instruction that his nonet can be played as chamber music or orchestrally. He recommends doubling the number of violas and cellos while sextupling the violins for an orchestral performance.

Several twentieth-century composers increased the number of string parts in orchestral music to achieve a dense texture. Penderecki in his *Threnody for the Victims of Hiroshima* uses 52 solo strings to create sound mass. Wallingford Riegger creates a similar texture in his *Study in Sonority*, which is scored for ten solo violins but can also be performed with multiple strings per part for a larger hall.

The majority of twentieth-century chamber works for large groups is for the mixed ensemble, which may include any combination of strings, winds, brass, percussion, and keyboard. Schoenberg's *Chamber Symphony*, Op. 9 (flute, oboe, English horn, two clarinets, bass clarinet, bassoon, contrabassoon, two French horns, and string quintet) contains the five-part string scoring of the late eighteenth century symphonies. Stravinsky's *Ragtime* (flute, clarinet, French horn, cornet, trombone, two percussion, two violins, viola, and double bass) is reminiscent of the divertimento ensemble of the 1770s with an even mix between winds and strings and the noted absence of the cello in the string choir. Twentieth-century nonets by Bohuslav Martinů and Alois Hába follow the scoring of the famous nineteenth-century works by Louis Spohr and Josef Rheinberger (woodwind quintet plus a quartet of strings) while Webern uses a more varied instrumentation. His two works for nine solo instruments, the *Sinfonia*, Op. 21 (four woodwinds, four strings, and harp) and the *Concerto*, Op. 24 (three woodwinds, three brass, two strings, and percussion) show a preference for new combinations.

The mixed ensemble has also lent itself well to the introduction of unusual instruments into the chamber music repertory. The electric guitar, an instrument we associate with rock combos appears in Sergio Cervetti's *Six Sequences for Dance* and George Wilson's *Concatenation*. The accordion, an instrument associated with dance and folk music, is featured in Hindemith's *Kammermusik No. 1* and Robert Gerhard's *Nonet*. The mandolin, seldom used in art music, appears in *Concerto* by Henryk Górecki.

The combination of voice and chamber ensemble is not new, but the single voice treated as just another "instrument" within the mixed ensemble, is a novel conception. Arnold Schoenberg in his *Pierrot Lunaire* of 1912 uses the vocal technique of *Sprechgesang* (half-speech and half-song) for reciting the text; there are five instrumentalists, three of whom double; eight different instruments are used. Peter Maxwell Davies and Harrison Birtwistle formed a chamber ensemble in 1967 called the "Pierrot Players." This group was based on the instrumentation of *Pierrot Lunaire* (flute doubling piccolo, clarinet doubling bass clarinet, violin doubling viola, piano, cello, and voice) with extra players added as required. Many of Davies' works were composed for the instrumentation of this chamber group.[59] George Crumb combines the use of *Sprechgesang* and the expandable ensemble in his *Songs, Drones, and Refrains of Death* (1969). The work is scored for baritone, electric guitar, electric double bass, electric piano, harpsichord, and two percussionists. Each performer is required to sing or whisper while playing his instrument.[60]

Boulez, in *Le Marteau sans Maître*, also treats the voice as another instrument within the ensemble, and, similar to the Schoenberg model, he writes some passages for the voice in *Sprechgesang* style. William Walton's *Façade*, although less serious in character, is also scored for voice and chamber ensemble. This composition is a "drawing-room entertainment" consisting of 21 brief poems by Edith Sitwell which are recited to the music of the ensemble in the manner of a melodrama.

Mixed media, the mixing of musical performance with other modes of artistic expression, such as dancing, acting, mime, film, and slides, were also effectively used with the chamber ensemble. Peter Maxwell Davies' chamber group, the "Fires of London," combines theater and concert elements. His *Eight Songs for a Mad King* is scored for voice and six instruments. The instrumentalists are dressed in costumes and perform musical as well as acting roles. Other chamber ensemble works by Davies that incorporate dramatic elements are *Revelation and Fall*, *Vesalii icones*, and *Miss Donnithorne's Maggot*.[61] One of the best known twentieth-century mixed media chamber works is Stravinsky's *L'Histoire du Soldat*, a conducting *tour de force* that combines dance, recitation, and music.

The large chamber ensemble has witnessed many changes in purpose, scoring, and sound from the eighteenth century to the present. Compositions for seven or more solo instruments in the eighteenth century were mostly functional music meant to entertain. Scoring for the works was either predominantly wind-dominated, for outdoor performances, or mixed winds and strings, similar to the scoring of the Classical symphony. The majority of nineteenth-century large chamber works were "mini-symphonies" in the form of nonets or dextets. Poised between chamber music as such and orchestral music, they resemble the early Romantic trios, quartets, quintets as well as symphonies in scope, style, and form. The emerging role of the winds and the blended colors of the larger Romantic orchestra are evident in these works. A small number of works written for specific occasions, to entertain, or for special functions, reminds us of the genres associated with the eighteenth-century *Divertimento* which served a similar purpose.

One of the most important musical developments of the twentieth century has been the Renaissance of the chamber ensemble. Composers have considered this ensemble, with the equal partnership of winds, strings, and percussion, ideal for expressing their renewed interest in the linear, contrapuntal style of writing. This modern "mixed consort," with novel combinations of instruments and sounds, has emerged as a major medium in twentieth-century music.

NOTES

1. Homer Ulrich, *Chamber Music*, 2nd ed., (New York: Columbia University Press, 1966), 7.

2. Robert Craft, "Performance Notes for Schoenberg's Quintet," *Woodwind Magazine* (June 1952): 6-7+.

3. *The New Harvard Dictionary of Music*, 1969 ed., s.v. "Chamber Music."

4. Ruth Halle Rowen, *Early Chamber Music*, 2d ed., 1949 (New York: Da Capo Press, 1974), 21.

5. Hubert Unverricht, "Divertimento," *The New Grove Dictionary of Music and Musicians*, ed. Stanley Sadie (London: Macmillian Pub. Ltd., 1980), vol. 5, 504-6.

6. Denis Arnold, "Concerto," *The New Oxford Companion to Music*, ed. Denis Arnold, (Oxford: Oxford University Press, 1983) vol. 1, 463.

7. Denis Arnold, "Concerto," *The New Oxford Companion to Music*, ed. Denis Arnold, (Oxford: Oxford University Press, 1983) vol. 1, 463.

8. Denis Arnold, "Chamber Music," *The New Oxford*, vol. 1, 345-6.

9. James Webster, "Towards a History of Viennese Chamber Music in the Early Classical Period," *Journal of the American Musicological Society* 27 (1974): 212.

10. Unverricht, "Divertimento," *The New Grove*, vol. 5, 505.

11. Webster, "Towards a History," 246.

12. Unverricht, "Divertimento," *The New Grove*, vol. 5, 504-5.

13. Sterling E. Murray, foreword to "Five Wind Partitas," by Antonio Rosetti, *Recent Researches in the Music of the Classical Era*, vols. 30-31, (Madison, Wis.: A-R Editions, Inc., 1989), viii-iv.

14. *The New Oxford Companion to Music*, 1983 ed., s.v. "Serenade."

15. Hubert Unverricht, "Serenade," *The New Grove*, vol. 17, 159-60.

16. *The New Oxford Companion to Music*, 1983 ed., s.v. "Cassation."

17. Hubert Unverricht, "Notturno," *The New Grove*, vol. 13, 431.

18. Marie K. Stolba, *The Development of Western Music: A History*, (Dubuque, Iowa: Wm. C. Brown Pub., 1990), 483.

19. Rowen, 140.

20. Unverricht, "Divertimento," *The New Grove*, vol. 5, 506.

21. Erik Smith, *Mozart Serenades, Divertimenti and Dances*, (London: BBC, 1982), 10-11.

22. Rowen, 163.

23. Ignaz Pleyel, *Periodical Symphonies*, ed. Raymond R. Smith, *Recent Researches in Music of the Classical Era*, (Madison, Wis.: A-R Editions, Inc., 1978), vol. 8, 1.

24. Rowen, 6.

25. Maddalena Laura Lombardini Sirmen, "Three Violin Concertos," ed. Jane L. Berdes, *Recent Researches in Music of the Classical Era*, (Madison, Wis.: A-R Editions, Inc., 1991), vol. 38, 1.

26. Wendy Thompson, "Sinfonia Concertante," *The New Oxford Companion*, vol. 2, 1778-9.

27. Barry S. Brook, "The Symphonie Concertante: An Interim Report," *The Musical Quarterly* 47 (1961): 503.

28. R. Larry Todd, "Orchestral Texture and the Art of Orchestration," *The Orchestra: Origins and Transformations*, ed. Joan Peyser, (New York: Charles Scribner's Sons, 1986), 205.

29. Michael Broyles, "Ensemble Music Moves Out of the Private House: Haydn to Beethoven," Peyser, ed. *The Orchestra*, 115.

30. Ibid., 102-3.

31. Robert L. Weaver, "The Consolidation of the Main Elements of the Orchestra: 1470-1768," Peyser, ed. *The Orchestra*, 28.

32. George B. Stauffer, "The Modern Orchestra: A Creation of the Late Eighteenth Century," Peyser, ed. *The Orchestra*, 53.

33. Michael Beckerman, "The New Conception of 'The Work of Art,'" Peyser, ed. *The Orchestra*, 347.

34. Gustav Schilling, *Universal-Lexikon der Tonkunst* (1835-1838), quoted in Alan Houtchens, "Romantic Composers Respond to Challenge and Demand," Peyser, ed. *The Orchestra*, 185.

35. Alan Houtchens, 185.

36. Adam Carse, *The Orchestra in the XVIII Century*, (New York: Broude Brothers Ltd., 1969), 21.

37. Ulrich, 242.

38. Jack Westrup, *Schubert Chamber Music*, (Seattle: University of Washington Press, 1969), 13.

39. Milton Cross and David Ewen, "Richard Strauss," *New Encyclopedia of the Great Composers and Their Music*, (Garden City, N.Y.: Doubleday & Company, Inc., 1969), vol. 2, 970-1.

40. Kurt Janetzky, foreword to *Marcia vivace* by Carl Maria von Weber, (Zürich: Albert Kunzelmann, 1984), 4.

41. Arnold Schoenberg, *Interview with Myself*, David Johnson, trans., in pamphlet accompanying Columbia Records M2L 294 (1962), quoted in Bryan R. Simms, "Twentieth-Century Composers Return to the Small Ensemble," Peyser, ed. *The Orchestra*, 459.

42. Ibid., 465-66.

43. Bryan R. Simms, 464.

44. Igor Stravinsky and Robert Craft, *Expositions and Developments* (1962), 102-3, quoted in Simms, 459.

45. Simms, 457.

46. Princess Edmond de Polignac, "Memoirs," *Horizon: A Review of Literature and Art*, 12 (1945), quoted in Simms, 462.

47. Simms, 463.

48. Igor Stravinsky and Robert Craft, 103-4, quoted in Simms, 461.

49. Simms, 461.

50. Charles E. Ives, *Memos*, ed. John Kirkpatrick (1972), quoted in Simms, 474.

51. Simms, 474.

52. Ibid., 474-5.

53. Ibid., 456.

54. Raoul Camus, "Bands," *The New Grove Dictionary of American Music*, ed. Stanley Sadie, (London: Macmillan Press Ltd., 1986), vol. 1, 133.

55. Reginald Smith Birdle, *Contemporary Percussion* (London: Oxford University Press, 1970), 1.

56. William P. Malm, *Music Cultures of the Pacific, the Near East, and Asia*, ed. H. Wiley Hitchcock, (Englewood Cliffs, N.J.: Prentice-Hall, Inc., 1967), 25-6.

57. Paul Earls and Richard Kassel, "Partch, Harry," *The New Grove Dictionary of American Music*, vol. 3, 482.

58. James Blades, *Percussion Instruments and Their History* (New York: Frederick A Praeger, Pub., 1970), 435.

59. Stephen Walsh, "Davies, Peter Maxwell," *The New Grove Dictionary of American Music*, vol. 5, 276.

60. David H. Cope, *New Directions in Music*, 4th ed., (Dubuque, Iowa: Wm. C. Brown Pub., 1984), 105.

61. Robert P. Morgan, *Twentieth-Century Music*, (New York: W.W. Norton & Co., 1991), 446.

THE REPERTORY

Compositions for 9 – 15 Instruments

Abrahamsen, Hans
1952

Geduldspiel
Fl, Ob, Cl, Hn, Trp, P, Vn, Va, Vc (9)
Wilhelm Hansen Musik-Forlag

Abrahamsen, Hans
1952

Lied in Fall
Afl/Pic, Ob/Eh, Cl, Bn, Hn, Trp, Trb, Per, P, 2 Vn, Va, Db (13)
Wilhelm Hansen Musik-Forlag

Abrahamsen, Hans
1952

Märchenbilder
Fl/Pic, Ob, Cl/Ecl, Bn, Hn, Trp, Trb, Per, P, 2 Vn, Va, Vc, Db (14)
Wilhelm Hansen Musik-Forlag

Adaskin, Murray
1906

Rondino for Nine Instruments
Fl, Ob, Cl, Bn, Hn, 2 Vn, Va, Vc (9)
Canadian Music Centre

Adler, Samuel
1928

Concert Piece
3 Trp, 2 Hn, 3 Trb, 2 Eu, Tba, Per (12)
Robert King Music Co.

Adler, Samuel
1928

Divertimento
3 Trp, 3 Hn, 3 Trb, 2 Eu, Tba (12)
Robert King Music Co.

Adler, Samuel
1928

Histrionics
4 Trp, 4 Hn, 4 Trb, Eu, Tba, P (15)
Southern Music Co.

Adler, Samuel
1928

Music for Eleven
2 Fl, Ob, Cl, Bcl, Bn, 5 Per (11)
Oxford University Press

2 A CONDUCTOR'S REPERTORY OF CHAMBER MUSIC

Adler, Samuel
1928

Praeludium
2 Trp, 2 Hn, 2 Trb, Eu, Tba, Per (9)
Robert King Music Co.

Aitken, Hugh
1924

Serenade
Fl, Ob, Cl, Bn, Hn, 2 Vn, Va, Vc, Db (10)
American Music Center

Akutagawa, Yasushi
1925-89

Music for Strings No. 1
4 Vn, 2 Va, 2 Vc, Db (9)
Ludwig Doblinger

Albright, William
1944

Marginal Worlds
Fl, Cl/Asx, Bn/Tsx, Trp, Trb, P, Vn, Va, Vc, Db, 2 Per (12)
Jobert & Cie

Alpaerts, Flor
1876-1954

Treurdicht
2 Trp, 4 Hn, 2 Bn, Per (9)
Centre Belge de Documentation Musicale

Alsina, Carlos
1941

Auftrag
Fl, Cl, Bn, Hn, Vn, Va, Vc, Db, Per (9)
Edizioni Suvini Zerboni

Alsina, Carlos
1941

Funktionen, Op. 14
Fl, Cl, Bn, Trp, P, 2 Per, Vn, Vc (9)
Edizioni Suvini Zerboni

Alwyn, William
1905-85

Fanfare for a Joyful Occasion
3 Trp, 4 Hn, 2 Trb, Tba, Per (11)
Oxford University Press

Amato, Bruno
1936

Basses and Brass
5 Trp, 4 Hn, 3 Db (12)
Seesaw Music Corp.

Ameller, André-Charles
1912

Fanfares pour Tous les Temps
4 Trp, 2 Hn, 4 Trb, Tba (11)
Alphonse Leduc

Ames, William
1901

Composition
Fl, Ob, Cl, Bn, Hn, 2 Vn, Va, Vc, Db (10)
American Composers Alliance

Anderson, Thomas
1928

Transitions
Fl, Cl, Bn, Hn, Trp, Trb, Vn, Va, Vc, P (10)
American Composers Alliance

Andriessen, Jurriaan
1925

Antifona e Fusione
Fl, Ob, Cl, Bn, 2 Hn, 2 Trp, Trb, Per (10)
Stichting Donemus

Andriessen, Jurriaan
1925

Concertino
2 Fl, 2 Ob, 2 Cl, 2 Bn, 2 Hn (10)
Stichting Donemus

Andriessen, Jurriaan
1925

Entrata Festiva
3 Trp, 4 Hn, 3 Trb, 2 Per (12)
Stichting Donemus

Andriessen, Jurriaan
1925

Hommage à Milhaud
Fl, Ob, Cl, Asx, Bn, Trp, Trb, Vn, Va, Vc (10)
Stichting Donemus

Andriessen, Jurriaan
1925

Respiration-Suite
2 Fl, 2 Ob, 2 Cl, 2 Bn, 2 Hn (10)
Stichting Donemus

Andriessen, Jurriaan
1925

Rouw Past Elektra...
Fl, 2 Ob, Cl, 2 Bn, Hn, 2 Trp, 2 Trb, Per (12)
Bärenreiter Verlag

Angerer, Paul
1927

Cogitatio
Fl, Ob, Cl, Bn, Hn, 2 Vn, Va, Vc, Db (10)
Ludwig Doblinger

Angerer, Paul
1927

Musica Articolata
2 Fl, 2 Ob, 2 Cl, 2 Bn, 2 Hn, Bcl, Trp, Trb (13)
Ludwig Doblinger

Antheil, George
1900-59

Ballet Méchanique
6 Per, 4 P (10)
Shawnee Press, Inc.

Antoniou, Théodore
1935

Concertino, Op. 21
Fl, Ob, 2 Cl, 2 Bn, 2 Hn, Trp, Per, P (11)
Bärenreiter & Neuwerk

Antunes, Jorge
1942

Intervertige
Fl, Ob, Cl, Bn, Hn, 2 Vn, Va, Vc, 2 Per (11)
Edizioni Suvini Zerboni

Apostel, Hans Erich
1901

Fischerhaus-Serenade, Op. 45
Fl, Ob, Cl, Bn, Hn, Trp, Trb, 2 Vn, Va, Vc, Db (12)
Ludwig Doblinger

Arnell, Richard
1917

Ceremonial and Flourish
3 Trp, 3 Hn, 3 Trb (9)
Associated Music Publishers

Arnell, Richard
1917

Ceremonial and Flourish, Op. 43
3 Trp, 4 Hn, 3 Trb (10)
Associated Music Publishers

Arnell, Richard
1917

Serenade, Op. 57
2 Fl, 2 Ob, 2 Cl, 2 Hn, 2 Bn, Db (11)
June Emerson-Wind Music

Arnold, Malcolm
1921

Trevelyan Suite, Op. 96
3 Fl, 2 Ob, 2 Cl, 2 Bn, 2 Hn (11)
G. Schirmer

Arrieu, Claude
1903-90

Dixtuor
2 Fl, Ob, 2 Cl, 2 Bn, Hn, Trp, Trb (10)
Billaudot Editions Musicales

Arrigo, Girolamo
1930

Fluxus, Op. 7
Fl, 2 Cl, Bn, Trp, Va, Vc, Db, Hp (9)
Aldo Bruzzichelli

Asioli, Bonifazio
1769-1832

Serenade
2 Vn, Fl, 2 Hn, Va, Bn, Db, P (9)
Fétis

Aubéry, Prudent-Louis
1796-1869

Grande Sérénade, Op. 48
Fl, 2 Cl, 2 Hn, Bn, 2 Vn, Va, Db (10)
Richault

Aubin, Tony
1907-81

Cressida Fanfare
3 Trp, 4 Hn, 3 Trb, 2 Eu, Tba, Per (14)
Alphonse Leduc

Aubin, Tony
1907-81

Vitrail
2 Fl, 4 Hn, 3 Trp, 3 Trb, Tba (13)
Alphonse Leduc

Autori, Franco
1903

La Senese '70
4 Vn, 2 Va, 2 Vc, Db (9)
Edizioni Suvini Zerboni

Babbitt, Milton
1916

Composition for 12 Instruments
Fl, Ob, Cl, Bn, Hn, Trp, Hp, Cel, Vn, Va, Vc, Db (12)
Associated Music Publishers

Babusek, Frantisek
1905-54

Noneto
Fl, Ob, Cl, Bn, Hn, Vn, Va, Vc, Db (9)
Slovensky Hudobny Fond

Baervoets, Raymond
1930-89

Fanfare Héroique & Fanfare Joyeuse
3 Trp, 4 Hn, 3 Trb, Tba, Per (12)
Muziekuitgaven Metropolis

Baervoets, Raymond
1930-89

Musica per 14 Strumenti
Fl, Ob, Cl, Bn, Hn, Bcl, Trp, Trb, Cel, Hp, Vn, Va, Vc, Db (14)
G. Ricordi & Co.

Baksa, Robert
1938

Nonet
Fl, Ob, Cl, Bn, 2 Vn, Va, Vc, Db (9)
Alexander Broude, Inc.

Balada, Leonardo
1933

Sonata for 10 Winds
Fl/Pic, Ob, Ecl, Bn, 2 Hn, 2 Trp, 2 Trb (10)
G. Schirmer

Balassa, Sándor
1935

Xenia-Nonet
Fl, Cl, Bn, Vn, Va, Vc, P, Hp, Per (9)
Editio Musica Budapest

Ballou, Esther Williamson
1915-73

Suite for Winds
2 Fl, 2 Ob, 2 Cl, 2 Bn, 2 Hn (10)
American Composers Alliance

Barber, Samuel
1910-81

Medea - Cave of the Heart
Fl/Pic, Ob, Cl, Bn, Hn, P, 2 Vn, Va, Vc, Db (11)
G. Schirmer

Barber, Samuel
1910-81

Mutations from Bach
3 Trp, 4 Hn, 3 Trb, Tba, Per (12)
G. Schirmer

Bartoš, Jan Zdeněk
1908

Divertimento I, Op. 79
Fl, 2 Ob, 2 Cl, 2 Hn, 2 Bsn (9)
Panton

Bassett, Leslie
1923

Nonet
Fl, Ob, Cl, Bn, Hn, Trp, Trb, Tba, P (9)
C.F. Peters Corp.

Bauer, Marion
1887-1955

Aquarelle Op. 39, No. 2
2 Fl, 2 Ob, 2 Cl, 2 Bn, 2 Hn, 2 Db (12)
American Composers Alliance

Bauer, Marion
1887-1955

Patterns, Op. 41, No. 2
2 Fl, 2 Ob, 2 Cl, 2 Bn, 2 Hn, Db (11)
American Composers Alliance

Bauszern, Waldemar von
1866-1931

Chamber Symphony
3 Vn, 3 Va, 3 Vc, Db, Org (11)
Willy Müller-Süddeutscher Musikverlag

Bax, Arnold
1883-1953

Nonett
Fl, Ob, Cl, Hp, 2 Vn, Va, Vc, Db (9)
Murdoch

Bäck, Sven-Erik
1919

Chamber Symphony
Fl, Cl, Bn, Hn, Trp, Trb, 2 Per, 3 Va, 2 Vc, Db (14)
Wilhelm Hansen Musik-Forlag

Beach, Bruce
1903-73

Fanfare and Chorale
3 Trp, 2 Hn, 3 Trb, 2 Eu, Tba (11)
Pro Musica Verlag

Beach, Bruce
1903-73

Five Intagli
4 Trp, 4 Hn, 3 Trb, Tba, Per (13)
Southern Music Co.

Beadell, Robert
1925

Introduction and Allegro
3 Trp, 3 Hn, 3 Trb, Eu, Tba, Per (12)
Robert King Music Co.

Beale, James
1924

Five Still Lifes, Op. 32
2 Fl/Pic, 2 Cl, Bcl, Bsn, Vc, Per, 2 Hp (10)
American Composers Alliance

Beck, Conrad
1901-89

Concerto
2 Fl, 2 Hn, P, 2 Vn, Va, Db (9)
Schott

Becker, Gunther
1924

Game for Nine
Fl, Cl, Bcl, Vn, Va, Vc, Gt, 2 Per (9)
Musikverlag Hans Gerig

Beckhelm, Paul
1906-66

Tragic March
4 Trp, 4 Hn, 3 Trb, Eu, Tba, Per (14)
Robert King Music Co.

Beckwith, John
1927

Circle with Tangents
Hpd, 7 Vn, 3 Va, 2 Vc, Db (14)
BMI Canada Ltd.

Bedford, David
1937

Trona for 12
Fl, Ob, Cl, Bn, 2 Trp, 2 Trb, 2 Vn, Va, Vc (12)
Universal Editions

Beethoven, Ludwig van
1770-1827

March in C Major
Fl, 2 Ob, 2 Cl, 3 Bn, 2 Hn, 2 Trp, Per (13)
Breitkopf & Härtel

Beethoven, Ludwig van
1770-1827

Twelve Contra Dances
Fl, 2 Ob, 2 Cl, 2 Bn, 2 Hn, 2 Vn, Vc, Db (13)
Schott & Company, Ltd.

Benes, Jiri
1928

Preference
Fl, Cl, Vn, Vc, Db, Hn, Trp, Hp, Gt (9)
Slovensky Hudobny Fond

Benguerel, Xavier
1931

Consort Music
6 Vn, 2 Va, 2 Vc, Db (11)
Edition Moeck

Benhamou, Maurice
1936

Mizmor-Chir
Fl, Hn, Trp, Trb, 3 Per, Vn, Va, Vc, Db (11)
Jobert & Cie

Bennett, Richard Rodney
1936

Jazz Calendar
Fl, Asx, T/Bsx, 2 Trp, Hn, Trb, Tba, P, Db, Per (11)
Universal Editions

Bentzon, Niels Viggo
1919

Chamber Concerto, Op. 52
Cl, 2 Bn, Trp, Db, Per, 3 P (9)
J. & W. Chester Ltd.

Bentzon, Niels Viggo
1919

Climate Changes, Op. 474
Bsx, P, Fl, Ob, Cl, Bn, Hn, Trp, Trb, Tba, Per, 2 Vn, Va, Vc (15)
Wilhelm Hansen Musik-Forlag

Bentzon, Niels Viggo
1919

Sinfonia Concertante, Op. 100
Cl, Vn, 3 Trp, 3 Trb, Tba, 2 Per (11)
Wilhelm Hansen Musik-Forlag

Bentzon, Niels Viggo
1919

Sonata for Twelve Instruments, Op. 257
Fl, Ob, Cl, Bn, Hn, Trp, Trb, P, Vn, Va, Vc, Db (12)
Wilhelm Hansen Musik-Forlag

Benvenuti, Arrigo
1925

Studi
Fl, Cl, Bn, Hn, Trp, Trb, Va, Vc, P, Per (10)
Aldo Bruzzichelli

Berger, Arthur
1912

Chamber Music
Fl, Ob, Cl/Bcl, Bn, Hn, Trp, 2 Vn, Va, Vc, Db, Cel, Hp (13)
C.F. Peters Corp.

Berkeley, Michael
1948

Chamber Symphony
Fl, Ob, Cl, Hn, P, Vn, Va, Vc (9)
Oxford University Press

Bernard, Jean Emile
1843-1902

Divertissement
2 Hn, Bn, 2 Cl, 2 Ob, 2 Fl (9)
Sansone

Bernard, Jean Emile
1843-1902

Divertissement, Op. 36
2 Fl, 2 Ob, 2 Cl, 2 Bn, 2 Hn (10)
Durand & Cie

Bertini, Henri
1798-1876

Nonett, Op. 107
P, Fl, Ob, Va, Vc, Hn, Bn, Trp, Db (9)
Henri Lemoine & Cie

Beversdorf, Samuel Thomas
1924-81

Cathedral Music
3 Trp, 4 Hn, 3 Trb, Eu, Tba (12)
Southern Music Co.

Beyer, Frank
1928

Concertino a Tre
2 Ob, Trp, Trb, P, 4 Vn, 2 Va, 2 Vc (13)
Bote & Bock

Beyer, Howard
1929

Suite for Brass Instruments
3 Trp, 4 Hn, 3 Trb, Per (11)
Robert King Music Co.

Bialas, Günther
1907

Partita
Fl, 2 Ob, 2 Cl, 2 Bn, 2 Hn, Db (10)
Bärenreiter & Neuwerk

Bialas, Günther
1907

Pastorale and Rondo
Fl, Ob, Cl, Bn, Hn, 2 Vn, Va, Vc, Db (10)
Bärenreiter Verlag

Bianchi, Gabriele
1901

Four Studi da Malu
Fl, Ob, Cl, Bn, Hn, Trp, 2 P, Per (9)
G. Ricordi & Co.

Bilik, Jerry
1933

Sonata for Brass
5 Trp, 4 Hn, 3 Trb, Eu, Tba, (14)
Samuel French, Inc.

Binkerd, Gordon
1916

Three Canzonas
3 Trp, 3 Hn, 3 Trb, Tba (10)
Boosey & Hawkes

Birtwistle, Harrison
1934

Tragoedia
Fl, Ob, Cl, Bn, Hn, 2 Vn, Va, Vc, Hp, Per (11)
Universal Editions

Birtwistle, Harrison
1934

Verses for Ensembles
Pic/Afl, Ob/Eh, Ecl/Cl, Cl/Bcl, Bn/Cbn, Hn, 2 Trp, 2 Trb, Per (13)
Universal Editions

Bland, William
1947

Sonics I, II, III
Trp, Hn, Trb, Tba, P, 2 Vn, Va, Vc (9)
Composer's Autograph Publications

Blank, Allan
1925

Paganini Caprice (XIV)
3 Trp, 4 Hn, 3 Trb, Tba (11)
American Composers Alliance

Blatter, Alfred
1937

Suite
4 Trp, 2 Hn, 2 Trb, Eu, Tba (10)
M.M. Cole Publishing Co.

Blickhan, Charles Timothy
1945

Variations/Permutations
Fl, Ob, Cl, Bn, Hn, Trp, Trb, P, 3 Per (11)
Seesaw Music Corp.

Bliss, Arthur
1891-1975

Fanfare for a Coming of Age
3 Trp, 4 Hn, 3 Trb, Tba, 2 Per (13)
Robert King Music Co.

Bliss, Arthur
1891-1975

Fanfare for the Lord Mayor of London
3 Trp, 4 Hn, 3 Trb, Tba, Per (12)
Robert King Music Co.

Bliss, Arthur
1891-1975

Fanfare, Homage to Shakespeare
5 Trp, 3 Trb, Tba, Per (10)
Robert King Music Co.

Bliss, Arthur
1891-1975

Music for 11 Strings
5 Vn, 3 Va, 2 Vc, Db (11)
Bärenreiter Verlag

Bliss, Arthur
1891-1975

The Women of Yueh
Fl, Ob, Cl, Bn, 2 Vn, Va, Vc, Db, 2 Per (11)
J. & W. Chester Ltd.

Bloch, Ernest
1880-1959

Four Episodes
Fl, Ob, Cl, Bn, Hn, 2 Vn, Va, Vc, Db, P (11)
Summy-Birchard Co.

Blum, Robert
1900

Musik
Fl, Cl, Hn, Bn, 2 Vn, Va, Vc, Db (9)
Sirius-Verlag

Boccherini, Luigi
1743-1806

Ouverture à Grand Orchestre, Op. 43
2 Ob, 2 Hn, Bn, Cbn, 2 Vn, 2 Va, Vc (11)
Fétis

Boeck, August de
1865-1937

Fanfare
3 Trp, 3 Hn, 3 Trb, 2 Per (11)
Scherzando

Boedijn, Gerard
1893-1972

5 Concertante Epigram-Schetsen, Op. 159
2 Fl, 2 Ob, 3 Cl, 2 Bn, 2 Hn, 2 Trp, P, Per (15)
Stichting Donemus

Boehm, Yohanan
1914

Divertimento
2 Fl, 2 Ob, 2 Cl, 2 Bn, 2 Hn (10)
Israeli Music Publishers

Boesmans, Philippe
1936

Explosives
Fl, Cl, 2 Vn, Va, Vc, Db, P, Hp, 2 Per (11)
Jobert & Cie

Bogusławski, Edward
1940

Intonazioni I
Fl, Cl, Trp, Trb, 2 Vn, Va, Vc, P (9)
Polskie Wydawnictwo Muzyczne

Böhner, Johann Ludwig
1787-1860

Serenade
Fl, Bn, 2 Hn, 2 Vn, Va, Vc, Db (9)
Boosey & Hawkes

Bois, Rob du
1934

Circle
2Cl, Tsx, Trp, Trb, Tba, Db, P, 3 Per (11)
Stichting Donemus

Bolcom, William
1938

Session IV
Cl, Trb, 2 Va, Vc, Hp, P, 2 Per (9)
Merion Music

Bon, Willem Frederik
1940-83

Passacaglia in Blue
2 Fl, 2 Ob, 2 Cl, 2 Bn, 2 Hn, Trp, Trb, Db (13)
Stichting Donemus

Bonneau, Paul
1918

Fanfare
3 Trp, 3 Hn, 2 Trb, Tba, Per (10)
Alphonse Leduc

Bonsel, Adriaan
1918

Folkloristische Suite
2 Fl, 2 Ob, 3 Cl, 2 Bn, 2 Hn, 2 Trp, Per (14)
Stichting Donemus

Bonvin, Ludwig
1850-1939

Romance, Op. 19a
Fl, 2 Ob, 2 Cl, 2 Bn, 2 Hn (9)
Boosey & Hawkes

Bořkovec, Pavel
1894-1972

Nonetto
Fl, Ob, Cl, Bn, Hn, Vn, Va, Vc, Db (9)
Editio Supraphon

Borstlap, Dick
1943

Fanfare II
Fl/Pic, 2 Asx, Tsx, Hn, Trp, 3 Trb, Db, P (11)
Stichting Donemus

Borstlap, Dick
1943

Over de Verandering
Fl, 2 Asx, Tsx, Hn, Trp, 3 Trb, Db, P (11)
Stichting Donemus

Bortolotti, Mauro
1926

Studio per Cummings No. 2
Ob, Cl, Pic/Cl/Bn, Bcl, Hn, 3 Per, Va, Vc, Db (11)
Edizioni Suvini Zerboni

Börtz, Daniel
1943

Kammarmusik
Fl, Cl/Bcl, Trp, Trb, Vn, Vc, 3 Per (9)
STIMS Informationscentral för Svensk Musik

Bottenberg, Wolfgang
1930

Variables
Fl/Pic, Ob, Cl, Bn, 2 Vn, Va, Vc, Db (10)
Canadian Music Centre

Bottje, Will Gay
1925

Serenade
Fl, Ob, Cl, Bn, Hn, 2 Vn, Va, Vc, Db (10)
Composers Facsimile Edition

Boykan, Martin
1931

Concerto
Fl/Pic, Ob, Cl, Bcl, Bn, Hn, Trp, Vn, Va, Vc, Db, P, Hp (13)
Boelke-Bomart Publications

Bozay, Attila
1939

Serie, Op. 19
Fl, Ob, Cl, Vn, Va, Vc, Db, P, Per (9)
Editio Musica Budapest

Bozay, Attila
1939

Sorozat
Fl, Ob, Cl, Vn, Va, Vc, Db, P/Hpd, Per (9)
Editio Musica Budapest

Božič, Darijan
1933

Concerto Grosso in F Major
Cl, Tsx, Trp, Trb, Db, P, 5 Per (11)
Edicije Društva Slovenskih Skladateljev

Bozza, Eugène
1905

Fanfare Héroique
3 Trp, 4 Hn, 3 Trb, Tba, Per (12)
Alphonse Leduc

Bozza, Eugène
1905

Messe Solennelle de Ste. Cécile
3 Trp, 4 Hn, 3 Trb, Tba, Per, Org (13)
Alphonse Leduc

Bozza, Eugène
1905

Overture pour une Cérémonie
3 Trp, 4 Hn, 4 Trb, Tba, Per (13)
Alphonse Leduc

Brandl, Johann
1760-1837

Grande Serenade, Op. 7
3 Vn, Ob, Vc, Bn, 2 Hn, Db (9)
Fétis

Brauer, Max
1855-1918

Pan
2 Fl, 2 Ob, 2 Cl, 2 Bn, 2 Hn, Db (11)
Boosey & Hawkes

Brautigam, Helmut
1914-42

Nonet, Op. 11
Fl, 2 Ob, 2 Cl, 2 Bn, 2 Hn (9)
Boosey & Hawkes

Brenta, Gaston
1902-69

Fanfare
3 Trp, 4 Hn, 3 Trb, Tba (11)
Centre Belge de Documentation Musicale

Brenta, Gaston
1902-69

Fanfare Héroique
3 Trp, 4 Hn, 3 Trb, Tba, Per (12)
Centre Belge de Documentation Musicale

Bresgen, Cesar
1913

Dorfmusikanten Op. 14
Fl, Ob, Trp, Trb, Per, 2 Vn, Vc, Db (9)
Willy Müller-Süddeutscher Musikverlag

Bresgen, Cesar
1913

Jagdkonzert
2 Fl, Ob, 2 Cl, 2 Bn, Hn, Db (9)
Schott & Company, Ltd.

Bresgen, Cesar
1913

Kammerkonzert, Op. 6
Fl, Cl, Hn, Vn, Va, Vc, Db, P, Per (9)
Willy Müller-Süddeutscher Musikverlag

Brian, William Havergal
1876-1972

Festival Fanfare
4 Trp, 4 Hn, 3 Trb, Tba (13)
Musica Viva

Britten, Benjamin
1913-76

Sinfonietta, Op. 1
Fl, Ob, Cl, Bn, Hn, 2 Vn, Va, Vc, Db (10)
Boosey & Hawkes

Brown, Earle
1926

Pentathis
Fl, Cl, Trp, Trb, Hp, P, Vn, Va, Vc (9)
B. Schotts' Söhne

Brown, Jonathan Bruce
1952

Fragments
Fl, Ob, Cl, Trp, Trb, 2 Vn, Va, Vc, P, Per (11)
American Composers Alliance

Brown, Newel
1932

Chant and Jubilee
Fl, 4 Hn, 4 Trp, 2 Trb, 2 Tba (13)
Seesaw Music Corp.

Brown, Rayner
1912

Passacaglia with Fugues
Fl, Afl, Ob, Eh, Cl, Bcl, Bn, Cbn, P (9)
Western International Music

Brugk, Hans Melchior
1909

Suite für 10 Blechbläser, Op. 8
3 Trp, 3 Hn, 3 Trb, Tba (10)
Heinrichshofen Verlag

Brumby, Colin James
1933

Fanfare
3 Trp, 4 Hn, 3 Trb, Tba, Per (12)
James Aebersold

Brün, Herbert
1918

Gestures for Eleven
Fl/Pic, Ob/Eh, Cl/Bcl, Bn/Cbn, Hn, Trp, Trb, Vn, Va, Db, Per, P (11)
Smith Publications

Brün, Herbert
1918

Passacaille, Op. 25
2 Fl, Ob, 2 Cl, Bn, 2 Hn, Db (9)
Henri Lemoine & Cie

Bubak, Josef
1902

Nonet, Op. 17
Fl, Ob, Cl, Bn, Hn, 2 Vn, Va, Vc, Db (10)
Panton

Bucchi, Thomas
1926

Battaglia
6 Trp, 2 Trb, Per (9)
Carisch S.P.A.

Buck, Ole
1945

Chamber Music I
Fl, Ob, Cl, Bn, Hn, Trp, 2 Vn, Va, Vc, Db (11)
Wilhelm Hansen Musik-Forlag

Buck, Ole
1945

Chamber Music II
Fl, Ob, Cl, Bn, Hn, 2 Vn, Va, Vc, Db (10)
Wilhelm Hansen Musik-Forlag

Bumcke, Gustav
1876-1963

Promenades, Op. 22
Fl, Ob, Eh, Cl, Acl, Hn, Bsx, Bn, Hp (9)
Andraud

Burghäuser, Jarmil
1921

Old Czech Fanfares
2 Trp, 4 Hn, 3 Trb, Per (10)
Robert King Music Co.

Burt, George
1929

Exit Music
Fl, Cl, Bcl, Hn, 2 Trb, Tba, 2 Per, Vn, Vc, Db (12)
Jobert & Cie

Busch, Adolf
1891-1952

Divertimento
Fl, Ob, Cl, Bn, 2 Hn, Trp, 2 Vn, Va, Vc, Per (12)
Andraud

Butting, Max
1888-1976

Hausmusik, Op. 119
Fl, Cl, 2 Vn, Vc, Trp, Gt, Per, Har (9)
VEB Deutscher Verlag

Büchtger, Fritz
1903-78

Concertino II
Fl, 2 Vn, Va, Vc, Db, 2 Per, P (9)
Gustav Bosse Verlag

Canning, Thomas
1911

Meditation for Strings
4 Vn, 2 Va, 2 Vc, Db (9)
Composers Facsimile Edition

Canning, Thomas
1911

Rondo
2 Trp, 2 Hn, 3 Trb, Tba, Per (9)
American Composers Alliance

Caplet, André
1878-1925

Suite Persane
2 Fl, 2 Ob, 2 Cl, 2 Bn, 2 Hn (10)
Manuscript Curtis I.

Cardon, Louis
1747-1805

Deux Concertos, Op. 10
2 Ob, 2 Hn, Hp, 2 Vn, Va, Db (9)
Fétis

Casanova, André
1919

Serenata
Fl, Cl, Bn, Trp, Trb, Per, Hp, 2 Vn, Va, Vc (11)
Billaudot Editions Musicales

Castillon de Saint-Victor, Alexis
1838-1873

Allegretto
Fl, Ob, Cl, Bn, Hn, 2 Vn, Va, Vc, Db (10)
Manuscript Fétis

Castro, Christobal de
1880

10 + 1
Fl, Ob, Cl, Hn, Trp, Trb, 2 Vn, Va, Vc, Per (11)
Editorial de Musica Española Contemporanea

Caturla, Alejandro
1906

Bembe
Fl, Ob/Eh, 2 Cl, Bn, 2 Vn, Va, Vc, Per, P (11)
Senart

Caturla, Alejandro
1906

Tres Danzas Cubanas
Fl/Pic, Ob/Eh, Cl, Bcl, Bn, 2 Hn, Trp, Trb, Tba, Per, P (12)
Elkan Vogel

Cazden, Norman
1914-80

Concerto for Ten Instruments
Fl, Ob, Cl, Bn, 2 Hn, Trp, P, Va, Vc (10)
MCA Music

Cazden, Norman
1914-80

Six Definitions
Cl, Eh, Hn, Trp, 2 Vn, Va, Vc, Db (9)
American Music Center

Cervelló, Jorge
1935

Catalisis
Fl, Ob, Cl, Bn, Eh, 2 Vn, Va, Vc, Db (10)
Editorial de Musica Española Contemporanea

Cervetti, Sergio
1940

Six Sequences for Dance
Fl, Hn, Cel, P, Vc, 5 Per, Egt (11)
Hermann Moeck Verlag

Chance, Nancy
1931

Darksong
2 Fl, 2 Cl, 2 Hn, Hp, Gt, P, 5 Per (14)
Seesaw Music Corp.

Charbonnier, Janine
1936

Systems
Cl, Bcl, Trp, Trb, Db, P, Om, 2 per (9)
E.F. M. Technisonor

Chaun, František
1921-81

Divertimento
Fl, 2 Ob, 2 Bcl, 2 Bn, 2 Hn (9)
Český Hudební Fond

Chávez, Carlos
1899-1978

Energía
Pic, Fl, Bn, Trp, Hn, Trb, Va, Vc, Db (9)
Belwin-Mills Company

Chávez, Carlos
1899-1978

Xochipilli
Pic, Fl, Ecl, Trb, 6 Per (10)
Belwin-Mills Company

Chemin-Petit, Hans
1902

Kleine Suite
Ob, Cl, Bn, Per, 2 Vn, Va, Vc, Db (9)
Lienau

Chemin-Petit, Hans
1902

Suite, Dr. Johannes Faust
Ob, Cl, Bn, Per, 2 Vn, Va, Vc, Db (10)
C.F. Peters Corp.

Chevreville, Raymond
1901-76

Divertissement, Op. 40
Fl, Cl, Bn, Hn, Hp, 2 Vn, Va, Vc, Db (10)
CeBeDem

Childs, Barney
1926

Jack's New Bag
Fl, Trp, Trb, P4h, 2 Per, Va, Vc, Db (10)
Composer/Performer Edition

Chou, Wen-Chung
1923

Soliloquy
2 Trp, 2 Hn, 3 Trb, Tba, Per (10)
C.F. Peters Corp.

Chou, Wen-Chung
1923

Two Miniatures from T'Ang
2 Fl, Cl, Hn, Vn, Va, Vc, Hp, P, Per (10)
American Composers Alliance

Chou, Wen-Chung
1923

Yu Ko
Vn, Afl, Eh, Bcl, 2 Trb, 2 Per, P (9)
C.F. Peters Corp.

Chou, Wen-Chung
1923

Yun
Fl, Cl, Bn, Hn, Trp, Trb, P, 2 Per (9)
C.F. Peters Corp.

Cianchi, Emilio
1833-1890

Nonetto
2 Ob, 2 Bn, 2 Cl, 2 Hn, Cbn (9)
Paoletti

Ciglic, Zvonimir
1921

Absurdi
Fl/Pic, Ob, Bn, Trp, Trb, 2 Vn, Va, Vc, Db (10)
Edicije Društva Slovenskih Skladateljev

Clementi, Aldo
1925

Concertino in forma di Variazioni
Fl, Ob, Bn, Cbn, Hn, Vn, Vc, Db, P (9)
Edizioni Suvini Zerboni

Clementi, Aldo
1925

Intermezzo
2 Fl, 2 Ob, 2 Cl, 2 Bn, 2 Hn (10)
Edizioni Suvini Zerboni

Clementi, Muzio
1752-1832

Sinfonia, Op. 44
2 Fl, 2 Ob, Bn, 2 Hn, 2 Vn, Va, Vc, Db (12)
G. Ricordi & Co.

Cobine, Albert
1929

Vermont Suite
4 Trp, 3 Hn, 4 Trb, Eu, Tba (13)
Robert King Music Co.

Cole, Hugo
1917

Serenade for Nine Wind Instruments
Fl, Ob, 2 Cl, 2 Bn, 2 Hn, Db (9)
Novello & Co., Ltd.

Constant, Marius
1925

Musique de Concert
Fl, Ob, Bn, Asx, Hn, Trp, Trb, 2 Per, P, Vn, Vc, Db (13)
Alphonse Leduc

Cooke, Arnold
1906

Sinfonietta
Fl, Ob, Cl, Bn, Hn, Trp, 2 Vn, Va, Vc, Db (11)
Belwin-Mills Company

Copland, Aaron
1900-90

Appalachian Spring Suite
Fl, Cl, Bn, 4 Vn, 2 Va, 2 Vc, Db, P (13)
Boosey & Hawkes

Copland, Aaron
1900-90

Ceremonial Fanfare
4 Hn, 3 Trp, 3 Trb, Tba (11)
Boosey & Hawkes

Copland, Aaron
1900-90

Fanfare for the Common Man
4 Trp, 4 Hn, 3 Trb, Tba, 2 Per (14)
Boosey & Hawkes

Copland, Aaron
1900-90

Nonet
3 Vn, 3 Va, 3 Vc (9)
Boosey & Hawkes

Cordero, Roque
1917

Paz-Paiz-Peace
Fl, Afl, Eh, Cl, Bcl, Bn, Vn, Va, Vc, Db, Hp (11)
Peer International

Corghi, Azio
1937

Actus I
2 Fl, 2 Ob, 2 Cl, 2 Bn, 2 Hn (10)
Edizioni Suvini Zerboni

Corghi, Azio
1937

Divertimento
Fl, Ob, Cl, Bn, Hn, Trp, Trb, Per, Vn, Va, Vc, Db (12)
CeBeDem

Cossart, Leland A.
1877

Suite
2 Fl, 2 Ob, 2 Cl, 2 Bn, 2 Hn (10)
Heinrichshofen Verlag

Cossart, Leland A.
1877

Suite, Op. 19
2 Fl, 2 Ob, 2 Cl, 2 Bn, 2 Hn, Hp (11)
Heinrichshofen Verlag

Cowell, Henry
1897-1965

Fanfare for the Forces of the Latin American Allies
3 Trp, 4 Hn, 3 Trb, Per (11)
Boosey & Hawkes

Cowell, Henry
1897-1965

Polyphonica
Fl, Ob, Cl, Bn, Hn, Trp, Trb, 2 Vn, Va, Vc, Db (12)
Associated Music Publishers

Crawford, John
1931

Three Palindromes
Fl, Bcl, Hn, Trp, 2 Vn, Va, Db, Per (9)
Composers Facsimile Edition

Creely, Robert
1926

Music for Ten Instruments
Pic, Cl, Cbn, Hn, Trp, Trb, Vn, Vc, Db, Hp (10)
American Composers Alliance

Crosse, Gordon
1937

Ariadne
Ob, Fl/Pic, Cl, Cl/Bcl, Trp, 2 Trb, Per, P/Cel, Vn, Va, Vc, Db (13)
Oxford University Press

Cunningham, Michael
1937

Spring Sonnet
Fl, 2 Cl, Asx, Tsx, Bcl, 3 Hn, Db (10)
Seesaw Music Corp.

Custer, Arthur
1923

Cycle for Nine Instruments
Fl/Pic, Bcl, Hn, Trp, Asx, Vn, Va, Vc, Db (9)
Joshua Corp.

David, Thomas
1925

Concerto for 9 Instruments
Fl, Ob, Cl, Bn, Hn, Vn, Va, Vc, Db (9)
Ludwig Doblinger

Davidovsky, Mario
1934

Inflexions
2 Fl, Cl, Trp, Trb, Per, P, Vn, Va, Vc, Db (11)
Edward B. Marks Music Corp.

Davidovsky, Mario
1934

Noneto
Fl, Ob, Cl, Bn, 2 Vn, Va, Vc, Db (9)
Edward B. Marks Music Corp.

Davies, Peter Maxwell
1934

Eram Quasi Agnus
Fl, Ob, Bsn, Cbn, Hn, 2 Trb, Hp, Per (9)
Boosey & Hawkes

Davis, Anthony
1951

Hemispheres
Fl, Cl, Trp, Trb, 3 Per, P, Vn, Vc, Db (11)
G. Schirmer

Davis, Anthony
1951

Wayang IV
Fl, Cl, Trb, 3 Per, Vn, Vc (9)
G. Schirmer

Debussy, Claude
1862-1918

Le Martyre de St. Sébastien Fanfares
4 Trp, 6 Hn, 3 Trb, Tba, Per (15)
Durand et Cie

Delas, José Luis de
1928

Imago
Fl, Afl, Cl, Bcl, P, Hp, Per, Vn, Va, Vc (10)
Hans Gerig Musikverlag

Delden, Lex van
1919-88

Fantasia, Op. 87
2 Ob, 2 Cl, 2 Bsn, 2 Hn, Hp (9)
Stichting Donemus

Delden, Lex van
1919-88

Nonet, Op. 101
Cl, Bn, Hn, 2 Vn, Va, Vc, Db, P (9)
Stichting Donemus

Delden, Lex van
1919-88

Sinfonia No. 7
2 Fl, 2 Ob, 2 Cl, 2 Hn, 2 Bn, Bcl (11)
Stichting Donemus

Denisov, Edison
1929

Music
Fl, 2 Ob, 2 Cl, 2 Bn, 2 Hn, Trp, Trb, Per (12)
C.F. Peters Corp.

Depelsenaire, Jean-Marie
1914

Divertissement Nocturne
2 Fl, 2 Vn, Va, Vc, Db, Trp, P (9)
Henry Lemoine & Cie

Devienne, Francois
1759-1803

Overture
2 Pic, 2 Ob, 2 Cl, 3 Bn, 2 Hn, Trb, Per (13)
Hofmeister Musikverlag

Devresse, Godfroid
1893-1972

Fanfare
3 Trp, 4 Hn, 3 Trb, Tba, Per (12)
Centre Belge de Documentation Musicale

Diamond, David
1915

Elegy in Memory of Maurice Ravel
3 Trp, 4 Hn, 3 Trb, Tba, Per, Hp (13)
Southern Music Pub. Co., Inc.

Diamond, David
1915

Nonet
3 Vn, 3 Va, 3 Vc (9)
Southern Music Pub. Co., Inc.

Diemente, Edward
1923

Love Song for Autumn
6 Trp, 4 Hn, 3 Trb, Tba (14)
Seesaw Music Corp.

Diemer, Emma Lou
1927

Declamation
2 Trp, 4 Hn, 2 Trb, Tba, Per (10)
Elkan-Vogel

Diemer, Emma Lou
1927

Declamation
4 Trp, 2 Hn, 2 Trb, Eu, Tba, 3 Per (13)
Elkan-Vogel

Ditters von Dittersdorf, Karl
1739-99

Concertino
2 Ob, Bn, 2 Hn, 2 Vn, 2 Va, Db (10)
Manuscript Traeg

Dobiáš, Václav
1909-78

O Rodne Zemi
Fl, Ob, Cl, Bn, Hn, Vn, Va, Vc, Db (9)
Artia

Dodge, Charles
1942

Folia
Fl, Ehn, Bcl, Tba, Vn, Va, P, 2 Per (9)
Boelke-Bomart Publications

Doležálek, Jan E.
1780-1858

Twelve Ecossaises
2 Vn, 2 Cl, 2 Hn, Fl, 2 Bn, Db (10)
Fétis

Donato, Anthony
1909

Nonet
3 Trp, 3 Trb, 3 Per (9)
Opus Music Publishers

Donatoni, Franco
1927

Lied
2 Fl, 2 Cl, 2 Vn, 2 Va, P, Hp, Per, Cel, Hpd (13)
Edizioni Suvini Zerboni

Donatoni, Franco
1927

Movimento
3 Fl, 2 Cl, Bn, 2 Hn, Trp, Hpd, P (11)
Edizioni Suvini Zerboni

Donatoni, Franco
1927

Solo per 10
5 Vn, 2 Va, 2 Vc, Db (10)
Edizioni Suvini Zerboni

Dondeyne, Désiré
1921

Trois Esquesses de Fanfare
3 Trp, 2 Hn, 3 Trb, Tba (9)
Editions Musicales Transatlantiques

Dost, Rudolf
1877

La Bal de Béatrice D'Este
2 Fl, 2 Cl, Ob, 2 Bn, 2 Hn, Trp, 2 Hp (12)
Northrup

Druckman, Jacob
1928

Incenters
Fl, Ob, Cl, Bn, Hn, Trp, Trb, P/Org, Vn, Va, Vc, Db, Per (13)
Belwin-Mills Company

DuBois, Robert
1934

Espace à Remplir Pour Onze Musiciens
2 Cl, Tsx, Trp, Trb, Tba, 2 Per, Db, P, (10)
Stichting Donemus

Dubois, Théodore
1837-1924

Dixtuor
Fl, Ob, Cl, Bn, Hn, 2 Vn, Va, Vc, Db (10)
Heugel & Cie

Dubois, Théodore
1837-1924

Nonetto
Fl, Ob, Cl, Bn, 2 Vn, Va, Vc, Db (9)
Heugel & Cie

Dufourt, Hugues
1943

Mura Della Citta Di Dite
Fl, Ob, Cl, Bcl, Hn, Trp, Trb, Hp, Cel, 2 Per (11)
Jobert & Cie

Dukas, Paul
1865-1935

Fanfare (La Peri)
3 Trp, 4 Hn, 3 Trb, Tba (11)
Durand et Cie

Durey, Louis
1888-1979

Interlude
4 Trp, 4 Hn, 3 Trb, Tba, Per (13)
Editions Musicales Transatlantiques

Dvořák, Antonin
1841-1904

Serenade, Op. 44
2 Ob, 2 Cl, 2 Bn, 2 Hn, Vc, Db (10)
Edwin F. Kalmus

Dzierlatka, Arié
1933

Melodies
Fl, Cl, Hn, Trp, P, Hp, Vc, 3 Per (10)
Edizioni Suvini Zerboni

Eaton, John
1935

Sonority Movement
Fl, 9 Hp (10)
Associated Music Publishers

Ebenhoh, Horst
1930

4 Scenes for 10, Op. 21, No. 1
Fl, Ob, Cl, Bn, Per, 2 Vn, Va, Vc, Db (10)
Ludwig Doblinger

Eckhardt, Sophie-Carmen
1899-1974

Nonet
Fl, Ob, Cl, Bn, Hn, Vn, Va, Vc, Db (9)
Canadian Music Centre

Edler, Robert
1934

Reflections
Cl, Vn, Va, Vc, Hn, Trb, P, 5 Per (12)
Edition Tonos

Edwards, George
1943

Bits
Fl, Ob, Cl, Bn, Vn, Va, Vc, Db, P, 2 Per (11)
American Composers Alliance

Edwards, George
1943

Uroboros
Fl, 2 Va, Vc, Cel, Hpd, Hp, Gt, Man (9)
American Composers Alliance

Egk, Werner
1901-83

Divertissement
Fl/Pic, 2 Ob, Cl, Cl/Bcl, 2 Hn, Bn, Bn/Cbn, Trp (10)
B. Schotts' Söhne

Egk, Werner
1901-83

Polonaise
Ob, Cl, Hn, Bn, 2 Vn, Va, Vc, Db (9)
B. Schotts' Söhne

Eichheim, Henry
1870-1942

Oriental Impressions
Fl, Ob, 4 Vn, Va, Hp, P, 2 Per (11)
B. Schotts' Söhne

Eisler, Hanns
1898-1962

Nonett No. 1
Fl, Cl, Bn, Hn, 2 Vn, Va, Vc, Db (9)
C.F. Peters Corp.

Eisler, Hanns
1898-1962

Nonette 2
Fl/Pic, Cl, Vn, Trp, 3 Vn, Db, Per (9)
Verlag Neue Musik

Eisler, Hanns
1898-1962

Ouvertüre Zu Einem Lustspiel
Fl, Cl, Bn, P, 2 Vn, Va, Vc, Db (10)
C.F. Peters Corp.

Eisma, Will
1929

If . . .
Fl, Ob, Cl, Bn, Hn, 2 Vn, Va, Vc, Db (10)
Stichting Donemus

Eller, Heino
1887-1970

Camera Eye
2 Asx, Vc, 2 P, 2 Gt, 2 Per (9)
Stichting Donemus

Enesco, Georges
1881-1955

Dixtuor
2 Fl, 2 Ob, 2 Cl, 2 Bn, 2 Hn (10)
Editions Salabert

Erb, Donald
1927

Fanfare
3 Trp, 2 Hn, 2 Trb, Tba, Per (9)
Theodore Presser

Erb, Donald
1927

Sonneries
4 Trp, 4 Hn, 3 Trb, Tba (12)
Merion Music

Erbse, Heimo
1924

Nonett, Op. 28
Ob, Cl, Bn, Hn, 2 Vn, Va, Vc, Db (9)
Hans Gerig Musikverlag

Erickson, Robert
1917

Chamber Concerto
Fl, Ob, Cl, Bn, Hn, Bcl, Trp, Trb, Vn, Va, Vc, Db, P, Hp (14)
Robert Erickson

Erod, Ivan
1936

Capriccio
2 Fl, 2 Ob, 2 Cl, 2 Bn, 2 Hn (10)
Ludwig Doblinger

Escher, Rudolf
1912-80

Sinfonia
Fl, Ob, Cl, Bn, Hn, 2 Vn, Va, Vc, Db (10)
Stichting Donemus

Etler, Alvin
1913-73

Concerto
Cl, 3 Trp, 3 Trb, 2 Db, 3 Per (12)
Associated Music Publishers

Farkas, Ferenc
1905

Kleine Turmmusik
3 Trp, 4 Hn, 2 Trb, Tba (10)
Boosey & Hawkes

Farrenc, Jeanne Louise
1804-75

Nonetto, Op. 38
Fl, Ob, Cl, Bn, Hn, Vn, Va, Vc, Db (9)
Fétis

Feld, Jindřich
1925

Kammersuite
Fl, Ob, Cl, Bn, Hn, Vn, Va, Vc, Db (9)
Alphonse Leduc

Feld, Jindřich
1925

Nonetto, Suite de Chambre
Fl, Ob, Cl, Bn, Hn, Vn, Va, Vc, Db (9)
Leduc

Feldman, Morton
1926

11 Instruments
Fl, Afl, Hn, Trp, Btrp, Vn, Vc, Trb, Tba, Per, P (11)
C.F. Peters Corp.

Feldman, Morton
1926

Ixion
3 Fl, Cl, Hn, Trp, Trb, P, Vc, Db (10)
C.F. Peters Corp.

Feldman, Morton
1926

Madame Press Died Last Week at 90
2 Fl, Hn, Trp, Trb, Tba, Cel, 2 Vc, 2 Db, Per (12)
Universal Editions

Feldman, Morton
1926

Numbers
Fl, Hn, Trb, Tba, Per, P/Cel, Vn, Vc, Db (9)
C.F. Peters Corp.

Feldman, Morton
1926

Projection 5
3 Fl, 3 Trp, 2 P, 3 Vc (9)
C.F. Peters Corp.

Fellagara, Vittorio
1927

Serenata
Fl, Cl, Bcl or Bn, P, Per, 2 Vn, Va, Vc (9)
Edizioni Suvini Zerboni

Ferrari, Luc
1929

Flashes
Pic, Ob, Cl, Bn, Hn, Trp, Trb, 2 Vn, Va, Vc, Db, Per (13)
Editions Musicales Transatlantiques

Ficher, Jacobo
1896-1978

Dos Poemas, Op. 10, No. 16 & 42
Fl, Ob, Cl, Bn, Hn, 2 Vn, Va, Vc, Db (10)
Fleischer

Finke, Fedelio
1891-1968

Suite, Musik für 11 Bläser
Fl, Ob, Cl, Bn, 2 Trp, 2 Hn, 2 Trb, Tba (11)
Breitkopf & Härtel

Finzi, Gerald
1901-56

A Severn Rhapsody
Fl, Ob, 2 Cl, Hn, Vn, Va, Vc, Db (9)
Andraud

Fisher, Stephen
1940

Music for Nine Instruments
Cl, Bn, Hn, Trp, Trb, Tba, Vn, Vc, Db (9)
MJQ Music, Inc.

Flagello, Nicholas
1928

Chorale and Episode
2 Trp, 4 Hn, 3 Trb, Tba (10)
General Music Publishing Co.

Flagello, Nicholas
1928

Concertino
2 Trp, 4 Hn, 3 Trb, Tba, P, Per (12)
General Music Publishing Co.

Flegier, Ange
1846-1927

Dixtuor in F Minor
Fl, Ob, Cl, Bn, Hn, 2 Vn, Va, Vc, Db (10)
Andraud

Fleming, Robert
1921-76

Maritime Suite
Fl, Ob, Cl, Bn, Hp, 2 Vn, Va, Vc (9)
Canadian Music Centre

Flosman, Oldřich
1925

Nonet No. 2
Fl, Ob, Cl, Bn, Hn, Vn, Va, Vc, Db (9)
Panton

Foerster, Josef
1859-1951

Nonet
Fl, Ob, Cl, Bn, Hn, Vn, Va, Vc, Db (9)
McGinnis & Marx

Folprecht, Zdeněk
1900

Concertino, Op. 21
Fl, Ob, Cl, Bn, Hn, Vn, Va, Vc, Db (9)
Artia

Fontyn, Jacqueline
1930

Pour Onze Archets
6 Vn, 2 Va, 2 Vc, Db (11)
G. Schirmer

Fortner, Jack
1935

Spring
Fl, Asx, Bn, Va, Vc, Db, Per, Hp, P (9)
Jobert & Cie

Françaix, Jean
1912

7 Danses d'après Les Malheurs de Sophie
2 Fl, 2 Ob, 2 Cl, 2 Bn, 2 Hn (10)
B. Schotts' Söhne

Françaix, Jean
1912

L'Heure Du Berger
Fl, Ob, 2 Cl, 2 Bn, Hn, Trb, P (9)
European American Music

Françaix, Jean
1912

Neuf Pièces Caractéristiques
2 Fl, 2 Ob, 2 Cl, 2 Bn, 2 Hn (10)
B. Schotts' Söhne

Françaix, Jean
1912

Sérénade
Fl, Ob, Cl, Bn, Hn, Trp, Trb, 2 Vn, Va, Vc, Db (12)
Cambridge Music Shop

Franco, Johan
1908-88

Fanfare
3 Trp, 3 Hn, 3 Trb (9)
American Composers Alliance

Franco, Johan
1908-88

The Pilgrim's Progress
Fl/Pic, Ob/Eh, Cl, Bn, 3 Trp, Trb, P, Per (10)
American Composers Alliance

Frankel, Ben
1906

Bagatelles (Cinque Pezzi Notturni)
Fl, Ob, Cl, Bn, 2 Vn, Va, Vc, Db, Hp (10)
Novello & Co., Ltd.

Frankel, Ben
1906

Bagatelles, Op. 35
Fl, Ob, Cl, Bn, Hn, Hp, 2 Vn, Va, Vc, Db (11)
Belwin-Mills Company

Freed, Isadore
1900-60

Symphony No. 2
4 Trp, 4 Hn, 3 Trb, 2 Tba (13)
Templeton Pub. Co., Inc.

Freedman, Harry
1922

Tsolum Summer
Fl, 3 Vn, 2 Va, Vc, Db, Per (9)
Canadian Music Centre

Fribec, Krešimir
1908

Danza di Gioja
Ob, Trp, Trb, 2 Vc, Db, P, 3 Per (10)
Edition Modern

Fribec, Krešimir
1908

Panta Rhei
Pic, Fl, Eh, Bcl, Va, Db, P, 3 Per (10)
Edition Modern

Frid, Géza
1904

Twelve Metamorphoses, Op. 54A
2 Fl, 2 Ob, 2 Cl, 2 Bn, Hn, P (10)
Stichting Donemus

Fritsch, Johannes
1941

Modulation II
Fl/Pic, Eh, Bcl, Trp, 2 Trb, 2 P, Per, Vn, Va, Vc, Db (13)
Feedback-Studio-Verlag

Froundberg, Ivar
1950

. . . en Vue de Roesnaes
Ob, 2 Cl, Trb, P, Cel, 2 Per, Va (9)
Wilhelm Hansen Musik-Forlag

Fundal, Kartsten
1966

Hoquetus
Fl, Ob, Cl, Bn, Hn, 2 Vn, Va, Vc, Db (10)
Wilhelm Hansen Musik-Forlag

Gabichvadze, Revaz
1913

Quick Motion
Fl, Ob, Cl, Bn, Hn, 2 Vn, Va, Vc (9)
Mezhdunarodnaya Kniga

Ganz, Rudolf
1877-1972

Brassy Prelude, Op. 31, No. 1
3 Trp, 4 Hn, 3 Trb, Tba (11)
Belwin-Mills Company

Ganz, Rudolf
1877-1972

Woody Scherzo for 13 Instruments
Pic, 2 Fl, 2 Ob, Eh, 2 Bn, Cbn, 3 Cl, Bcl (13)
Mills

Geissler, Fritz
1921-84

Nonett
Fl, Ob, Cl, Bn, Hn, Vn, Va, Vc, Db (9)
VEB Deutscher Verlag

Geissler, Fritz
1921-84

Ode an eine Nachtigall
Fl, Ob, Cl, Bn, Hn, 2 Vn, Va, Vc (9)
Deutscher Verlag fur Musik

Gentilucci, Armando
1939

Fantasia No. 2
Fl, 4 Vn, 2 Va, 2 Vc, Db, Per (11)
Edizioni Suvini Zerboni

Gentilucci, Armando
1939

Rifrazioni per 10
5 Vn, 2 Va, 2 Vc, Db (10)
Edizioni Suvini Zerboni

Genzmer, Harold
1909

Nonett
Ob, Cl, Bn, Hn, 2 Vn, Va, Vc, Db (9)
C.F. Peters Corp.

Geraedts, Jaap
1924

Koraal-Fanfare
3 Trp, 4 Hn, 3 Trb, Tba, Per (12)
Stichting Donemus

Gerhard, Roberto
1896-1970

Hymnody
Fl, Ob, Cl, Hn, Trp, Trb, Tba, 2 P, Per (10)
Oxford University Press

Gerhard, Roberto
1896-1970

Hymnody
Fl, Ob, Cl, Hn, Trp, Trb, Tba, 2 P, 2 Per (11)
Oxford University Press

Gerhard, Roberto
1896-1970

Leo
Fl/Pic, Cl, Hn, Trp, Vn, Vc, P, Cel, 2 Per (10)
Oxford University Press

Gerhard, Roberto
1896-1970

Nonet
Fl, Ob, Cl, Bn, Hn, Trp, Trb, Tba, Acc (9)
Belwin-Mills Company

Gerschefski, Edwin
1909

Prelude
Pic, Fl, Ob, Eh, Cl, Bcl, Hn, Hp, 3 Per (11)
American Composers Alliance

Gibson, Jon Charles
1940

Melody IV
Asx, Trb, 2 Org, Vn, Va, Vc, Db, Per (9)
American Music Center

Giefer, Willy
1930

Pro-Kontra
Fl/Pic, Ob, Cl, Bn, Hn, Per, Vn, Va, Vc, Db (10)
Musikverlag Hans Gerig

Gilbert, Anthony
1934

Brighton Piece
Ecl, Cl, Bcl, Hn, Trp, Trb, Vc, 4 Per (11)
B. Schotts' Söhne

Gilse, Jan van
1881-1944

Nonet
Ob, Cl, Bn, Hn, 2 Vn, Va, Vc, Db (9)
Stichting Donemus

Giuranna, Bruno
1933

Adagio e Allegro Da Concerto
Fl, Ob, Cl, Bn, Hn, Vn, Va, Vc, Db (9)
G. Ricordi & Co.

Glass, Philip
1937

Glassworks
2 Fl, Ssx, Tsx, 2 Hn, P, Va, Vc (9)
Dunvagen Music Pub. Inc.

Glazounov, Alexander
1865-1936

Fanfares
2 Trp, 4 Hn, 3 Trb, Tba, Per (11)
Luck's Music Library

Godron, Hugo
1900-71

Amabile-Suite
Cl, 2 Vn, Va, Vc, 2 Vn, Va, Vc, Db, P (11)
Stichting Donemus

Goeyvaerts, Karel
1923

Op. 2
Pic, 2 Ob, 2 Bcl, P, 2 Vn, 2 Va, 2 Vc, Db (12)
CeBeDem

Goldman, Edwin Franco
1878-1956

March for Brasses
3 Trp, 2 Hn, 3 Trb, Eu, Tba, Per (11)
Chappel & Co., Inc.

Goldman, Richard Franco
1910

Hymn for Brass Choir
4 Trp, 4 Hn, 3 Trb, Eu, Tba, Per (14)
Robert King Music Co.

Goodenough, Forrest
1918

Fanfarce
3 Trp, 4 Hn, 3 Trb, Tba (11)
American Composers Alliance

Goossens, Eugene
1893-1962

Fantasy for Nine Wind Instruments
Fl, Ob, 2 Cl, 2 Bn, 2 Hn, Trp (9)
Curwen

Goossens, Eugene
1893-1962

Petite Symphonie
Fl, 2 Ob, 2 Cl, 2 Bn, 2 Hn (9)
Costallat

Górecki, Henryk Mikolaj
1933

Concerto, Op. 11
Fl, Cl, Trp, Per, Man, 2 Vn, Va, Vc (9)
Polskie Wydawnictwo Muzyczne

Górecki, Henryk Mikolaj
1933

Genesis, Op. 19, No. 2
Trp, Fl, 2 Per, 2 P, 2 Vn, 3 Va, Pic, Gt, Man (14)
Ars Polona

Górecki, Henryk Mikolaj
1933

Muzyczka 2
4 Trp, 4 Trb, Per, 2 P (11)
Polskie Wydawnictwo Muzyczne

Görner, Hans-Georg
1908

Intrada et Hymnus, Op. 20
3 Trp, 3 Hn, 3 Trb (9)
Heinrichshofen Verlag

Gounod, Charles
1818-93

Petite Symphonie
Fl, 2 Ob, 2 Cl, 2 Hn, 2 Bn (9)
Billaudot Editions Musicales

Gouvy, Louis
1819-98

Petite Suite Gauloise, Op. 90
Fl, 2 Ob, 2 Cl, 2 Bn, 2 Hn (9)
Universal Editions

Grabner, Hermann
1886-1969

Perkeo Suite for Wind Orch., Op. 15
2 Fl, 2 Ob, 2 Cl, 3 Bn, 4 Hn, Per (14)
Kahnt

Grandert, Johann
1939

Nonett
Fl, Ob, Cl, Bn, Hn, Trp, Trb, Bsx, Vc (9)
STIMS Informationscentral för Svensk Musik

Grant, Parks
1910

Prelude and Dance, Op. 39
3 Trp, 4 Hn, 3 Trb, Tba (11)
Composers Facsimile Edition

Grimm, Carl Hugo
1890-1978

Byzantine Suite
Fl, Ob, Cl, Bn, Hn, Trp, 2 Vn, Va, Vc, Db (11)
Andraud

Grovlez, Gabriel
1879-1944

Nocturne
Fl, 2 Ob, 2 Cl, 2 Bn, 2 Hn (9)
Sansone

Gruber, Heinz
1943

Revue for 10 Instruments
Fl, Ob, Cl, Bn, Hn, 2 Vn, Va, Vc, Db (10)
Ludwig Doblinger

Guaccero, Domenico
1927

. . . un iter segnato
Ob, Cl, Bn, Trp, Trb, 2 Vn, Va, Vc, Db (10)
Aldo Bruzzichelli

Gudmundsen-Holmgreen, Pell
1932

Two Improvisations
Fl, Cl, Hn, Trp, Trb, Db, P, 3 Per (10)
The Society for Publishing Danish Music

Guézec, Jean-Pierre
1934-71

Concert en 3 Parties
Fl, Ob, Cl, Bn, 2 Vn, Va, Vc, Db, P, Per (11)
Editions Salabert

Guinjoàn, Juan
1931

Fragment
Fl, Ob, Cl, Bn, Trp, P, 2 Vn, Va, Vc, Per (11)
Editorial de Musica Española Contemporanea

Guinjoàn, Juan
1931

Improvisation I
Pic/Fl, Ob, Cl, P, Vn, Va, Vc, Db, 2 Per (10)
Editorial Alpuerto

Gwilt, David
1932

Suite for Woodwind & Brass Instruments
2 Fl, Ob, 2 Cl, Cbn, 2 Trp, 2 Hn, 2 Trb, Per (13)
Novello & Co., Ltd.

Hába, Alois
1893-1973

Nonet No. 1, Op. 40
Fl, Ob, Cl, Bn, Hn, Vn, Va, Vc, Db (9)
Musikverlag Hans Gerig

Hába, Alois
1893-1973

Nonet No. 3, Op. 82
Fl, Ob, Cl, Bn, Hn, Vn, Va, Vc, Db (9)
Artia

Haddad, Donald
1935

Fugue in D Minor
3 Trp, 3 Hn, 3 Trb, Tba, Per (11)
Shawnee Press, Inc.

Hahn, Reynaldo
1874-1947

La Bal de Béatrice D'Este
2 Fl, 2 Cl, Ob, 2 Bn, 2 Hn, Trp, Per, 2 Hp, 2 Per (15)
Fleischer

Hamilton, Ian
1922

Windflowers
Hp, Fl/Eh, Cl, Hn, Trp, Per, Vn, Va, Vc (10)
Theodore Presser

Harbison, John
1938

Confinement
Fl, Ob/Eh, Cl/Bcl, Asx, Trp, Trb, Per, P, Vn, Va, Vc, Db (12)
Associated Music Publishers

Hardin, Burton
1936

Regal Festival Music
3 Trp, 4 Hn, 3 Trb, Eu, Tba (12)
Composer's Autograph Publications

Harper, Edward
1941

Ricercare
Fl, Cl, Bcl, Hn, Trp, Vn, Va, Db, P, Hp, Per (11)
Oxford University Press

Harris, Donald
1931

Ludus I
Fl, Ob, Cl, Bn, Hn, 2 Vn, Va, Vc, Db (10)
Jobert & Cie

Harris, Donald
1931

Ludus, Chamber Concerto
Fl, Ob, Cl, Hn, Bn, 2 Vn, Va, Vc, Db (10)
Elkan-Vogel

Harris, Russell
1914

3 Three-Parts
4 Trp, 3 Hn, 3 Trb, Eu, Tba (12)
American Composers Alliance

Harsányi, Tibor
1898-1954

L'Histoire du Petit Tailleur
Fl, Cl, Bn, Trp, Vn, Vc, P, 4 Per (11)
Durand & Cie

Harsányi, Tibor
1898-1954

Nonett
Fl, Ob, Cl, Bn, Hn, 2 Vn, Va, Vc (9)
Andraud

Hartley, Walter
1927

Double Concerto
Fl, Ob, Cl, Bn, Hn, Asx, Tba, 2 Trp, Trb (10)
Artisan Music Press

Hartley, Walter
1927

Sinfonia No. 3
5 Trp, 4 Hn, 3 Trb, Eu, Tba (14)
Tenuto Publications

Hartmann, Emil
1836-1898

Serenade, Op. 43
Fl, Ob, 2 Cl, 2 Hn, 2 Bn, Vc, Db (10)
Ries & Erler

Hasquenoph, Pierre
1922

Divertissement
Fl, Ob, Cl, Bn, Hn, 2 Vn, Va, Db (9)
Ludwig Doblinger

Hasquenoph, Pierre
1922

Divertissement pour Dixtuor
Fl, Ob, Cl, Bn, Hn, 2 Vn, Va, Vc, Db (10)
Ludwig Doblinger

Hauer, Josef
1883-1959

Dance Suite No. 1, Op. 70
Fl, Ob, Cl, Bn, P, 2 Vn, Va, Vc (9)
Universal Editions

Hauer, Josef
1883-1959

Dance Suite No. 2, Op. 71
Fl, Ob, Bcl, Bn, P, 2 Vn, Va, Vc (9)
Universal Editions

Hauer, Josef
1883-1959

Zwölftonspiel
Fl, Ob, Bcl, Bn, 2 Vn, Va, Vc, P4h (10)
Ludwig Doblinger

Hauer, Josef
1883-1959

Zwölftonspiel
Fl, Cl, Bcl, Bn, 2 Vn, Va, Vc, P (9)
Ludwig Doblinger

Haydn, Franz Joseph
1732-1809

Cassation, Hob. II:C3
2 Hn, 2 Ob, 2 Fl, 2 Bn, 2 Vn, Db (11)
Breitkopf & Härtel

Haydn, Franz Joseph
1732-1809

Cassazione, No. 2 in G Major, Hob. II:G1
2 Vn, 2 Va, Db, 2 Hn, 2 Ob (9)
Fétis

Haydn, Franz Joseph
1732-1809

Cassazione, No. 3 in G Major, Hob. II:9
2 Vn, 2 Va, Db, 2 Hn, 2 Ob (9)
Fétis

Haydn, Franz Joseph
1732-1809

Divertimento in D Major
3 Vn, 2 Hn, 2 Ob, Va, Fl, Vc, Bn, Db (13)
Breitkopf & Härtel

Haydn, Franz Joseph 1732-1809	Divertissement In D Major, Hob. II:8 2 Vn, 2 Va, Db, 2 Hn, 2 Ob (9) Fétis
Haydn, Franz Joseph 1732-1809	Divertissement No. 1 in F Major, Hob. II:20 2 Vn, 2 Va, Db, 2 Hn, 2 Ob (9) Fétis
Haydn, Franz Joseph 1732-1809	Divertissement No. 2 in F Major 2 Vn, 2 Fl, 2 Hn, 2 Bn, Db (9) Fétis
Haydn, Franz Joseph 1732-1809	Eight Nocturnes, Hob. II:25-32 2 Hn, 2 Lo, 2 Cl, 2 Va, Db (9) Pohl
Haydn, Franz Joseph 1732-1809	Feldpartitur, Chorale St. Antoine, Hob. II:46 2 Ob, 2 Cl, 2 Hn, 3 Bn, Cbn (10) Schuberth Verlag
Haydn, Franz Joseph 1732-1809	Nocturne, No. 5 in C Major, Hob. II:29 Fl, Ob, 2 Vn, 2 Va, 2 Hn, Db (9) Pohl
Haydn, Franz Joseph 1732-1809	Nocturne, No. 6 in G Major, Hob. II:30 Fl, Ob, 2 Vn, 2 Hn, 2 Va, Db (9) Pohl
Haydn, Franz Joseph 1732-1809	Nocturne, No. 7 in C Major, Hob. II:31 Fl, Ob, 2 Vn, 2 Va, Db, 2 Hn (9) Schmid
Haydn, Franz Joseph 1732-1809	Nonet, No. 20 2 Ob, 2 Hn, 2 Vn, Va, Vc, Db (9) Geiringer
Haydn, Franz Joseph 1732-1809	Notturno I in C Major, Hob. II:25 Fl, Ob, 2 Hn, 2 Vn, 2 Va, Vc, Db (10) Schmid
Haydn, Franz Joseph 1732-1809	Notturno II in C Major 2 Fl, 2 Hn, 2 Vn, 2 Va, Vc, Db (10) Schmid
Haydn, Franz Joseph 1732-1809	Notturno II in F Major, Hob. II:26 Fl, Ob, 2 Hn, 2 Vn, 2 Va, Vc, Db (10) Schmid
Haydn, Franz Joseph 1732-1809	Notturno V in C Major, Hob. II:29 Fl, Ob, 2 Hn, 2 Vn, 2 Va, Vc, Db (10) Universal Editions

Haydn, Franz Joseph
1732-1809

Partita in F Major
Fl, Ob, 2 Hn, 2 Vn, 2 Va, Vc, Db (10)
Universal Editions

Haydn, Franz Joseph
1732-1809

Two Marches, Hob. VIII:1&2
2 Cl, 2 Bn, Ser, 2 Hn, 2 Trp (9)
Fleischer

Hazell, Chris
1948

3 Brass Cats
Hn, 4 Trp, 4 Trb, Tba (10)
Chester Music Limited

Hazell, Chris
1948

Kraken
Hn, 4 Trp, 4 Trb, Tba (10)
Chester Music Limited

Hazzard, Peter
1949

Mentor
4 Trp, 4 Hn, Tba, 4 Per (13)
Seesaw Music Corp.

Hechtel, Herbert
1937

Trial
Fl, Cl, Trb, Vn, Va, Vc, P, 2 Per (9)
Hans Gerig Musikverlag

Hedwall, Lennart
1932

Partita
2 Fl, 2 Ob, 2 Cl, 2 Bn, 2 Hn, 2 Trp, Trb (13)
STIMS Informationscentral för Svensk Musik

Heider, Werner
1930

Sonatina
Fl, Cl, Tsx, Hn, Trb, Hp, P, Db, 2 Per (10)
MJQ Music, Inc.

Hemel, Oscar van
1892

Divertimento No. 2
2 Fl, 2 Ob, 2 Cl, 2 Bn, 2 Hn, 2 Trp, P (13)
Stichting Donemus

Henkemans, Hans
1913

Primavera
Fl, Ob, 3 Vn, 2 Va, Vc, Db (9)
Stichting Donemus

Henze, Hans Werner
1926

In Memoriam Die Weisse Rose
Fl, Ob, Cl, Bn, Hn, Trp, Trb, 2 Vn, Va, Vc, Db (12)
Cambridge Music Shop

Herberigs, Robert
1886-1974

Suite No. 1
3 Trp, 4 Hn, 3 Trb (10)
Centre Belge de Documentation Musicale

Herberigs, Robert
1886-1974

Suite No. 2
3 Trp, 4 Hn, 3 Trb (10)
Centre Belge de Documentation Musicale

Hespos, Hans-Joachim
1938

Break
Ob, 2 Trp, Fn, Tsx, Bsx, Trb, P, Vc, Db, Per (11)
Edition Modern

Hespos, Hans-Joachim
1938

Keime und Male
Pic, Fl, 2 Cl, Asx, Hn, Gt, Vn, Va, Db, 3 Per (13)
Jobert & Cie

Hespos, Hans-Joachim
1938

Passagen
Cl/Ecl, Asx, Trp, Trb, Va, Db, 4 Per (10)
Edition Modern

Hess, Willy
1906

Serenade, Op. 19
Fl, Ob, Cl, 2 Bn, 2 Hn, 2 Vn, Va, Vc (11)
Eulenburg

Hess, Willy
1906

Suite, Op. 53
2 Fl, 2 Ob, 2 Cl, 2 Bn, 2 Hn, Trp, Trb (12)
Breitkopf & Härtel

Heussenstam, George
1926

Seventeen Impressions from the Japanese, Op. 35
Fl, Ob, Cl, Hn, 6 Per, Vn, Va, Vc, Db (14)
Seesaw Music Corp.

Heussenstam, George
1926

Two Fanfares
5 Trp, 4 Trb (9)
Seesaw Music Corp.

Hétu, Jacques
1938

Cycle, Op. 16
Fl, Cl, Bcl, Bn, Hn, 2 Trp, 2 Trb, P (10)
Canadian Music Centre

Hibbard, William
1939

Four Pieces
Fl, Cl, Hn, Trb, Vn, Db, P, 2 Per (9)
American Composers Alliance

Hibbard, William
1939

Sensuous Extractions
Fl, Cl, Hn, Trb, Vn, Db, P, 2 Per (9)
American Music Center

Hibbard, William
1939

Stabiles
Fl, Afl, Cl/Ecl, Bcl, Trp, Trb, Per, Hp, P, Vn, Va, Vc, Db (13)
Associated Music Publishers

Hibbard, William
1939

Variations for Brass Nonet
3 Trp, 3 Hn, 3 Trb (9)
MJQ Music Inc.

Hiller, Johann Adam
1728-1804

Divertimento
2 Hn, 2 Ob, 2 Fl, 2 Vn, Db (9)
Breitkopf & Härtel

Hiller, Lejaren 1924	Divertimento Pic, Fl, Ob, Cl, Bn, Hn, Trp, Trb, Db, Gt, 2Per (12) Theodore Presser
Hindemith, Paul 1895-1963	Concert Music, Op. 36, No. 1 Fl, Ob, Cl, Bcl, Bn, Hn, Trp, Trb, Vn, Va, Vc, Db, P (13) Andraud
Hindemith, Paul 1895-1963	Concert Suite, Op. 28 Fl, Cl, Hn, Trp, 2 Vn, Va, Vc, Db (9) Cambridge Music Shop
Hindemith, Paul 1895-1963	Kammermusik No. 3 Afl/Pic, Ob, 2 Cl, Bn, Hn, Trb, Vc, Db (9) Schott & Company, Ltd.
Hindemith, Paul 1895-1963	Kammermusik, Op. 24, No. 1 Fl, Cl, Bn, Trp, Per, P, 2 Vn, Va, Vc, Db, Acc (12) B. Schotts' Söhne
Hindemith, Paul 1895-1963	Kammermusik, Op. 3 Fl, Cl, Ob, Bn, Trp, Trb, Vn, 2 Vc, Db (11) Schott & Company, Ltd.
Hlobil, Emil 1901	Nonet, Op. 27 Fl, Ob, Cl, Bn, Hn, Vn, Va, Vc, Db (9) Artia
Hoch, Francesco 1943	L'Oggetto Disincantato Fl, Ob, Cl, Bn, Hn, Trp, Trb, P, Hpd, Vn, Va, Vc, Db (13) Edizioni Suvini Zerboni
Hoch, Francesco 1943	Transparenza per Nuovi Elementi Fl, Ob, Cl, Bcl, Vn, Va, Vc, Db, P, Per (10) Edizioni Suvini Zerboni
Hodeir, André 1921	Ambiquite I Fl, Ecl, Cl, Bn, Hn, Trb, Hp, P, Db, 2 Per (11) MJQ Music, Inc.
Hodkinson, Sydney 1934	Valence 8 Vn, 2 Va, 2 Vc, Db (13) Jobert & Cie
Hoffmeister, Franz Anton 1754-1812	Serenade 2 Ob, 2 Cl, 2 Hn, 2 Bn, Db (9) N. Simrock
Hogg, Merle 1922	Concerto 3 Trp, 3 Hn, 3 Trb, Eu, Tba, Per (12) Robert King Music Co.

Hogg, Merle
1922

Sonata
4 Trp, 3 Hn, 3 Trb, Eu, Tba (12)
Standard Music Publishers

Holbrooke, Josef
1878-1958

Nocturne
2 Fl, 2 Ob, Eh, 2 Cl, 2 Bn (9)
Andraud

Holloway, Robin
1943

Concertino No. 3
Fl, Cl, Bn, Asx, Trp, Hn, Trb, 2 Vn, 2 Per (11)
Boosey & Hawkes

Holloway, Robin
1943

Divertimento
Fl/Pic, 2 Ob, 2 Cl, 2 Hn, 2 Bn (9)
Boosey & Hawkes

Holmboe, Vagn
1909

Chamber Concerto No. 2, Op. 20
Fl, 3 Vn, Va, Vc, Db, 2 Per, Cel (10)
The Society for Publishing Danish Music

Homs, Joaquin
1906

Musica Para 11
Fl, Ob, Cl, Trp, Trb, P, Per, 2 Vn, Va, Vc (11)
Editorial Alpuerto

Honegger, Arthur
1892-1955

Pastorale d'Eté
Fl, Ob, Cl, Bn, Hn, 2 Vn, Va, Vc, Db (10)
Andraud

Horvath, Josef
1931

Sothis I
Fl/Pic, Ob/Eh, Cl, Bcl, Bn, Hn, Trp, Trb, 2 Vn, Va, Vc, Db (13)
Ludwig Doblinger

Hovhaness, Alan
1911

Mountains and Rivers Without End
Fl, Ob, Cl, Trp, Trb, Tba, 3 Per, Hp (10)
C.F. Peters Corp.

Hovhaness, Alan
1911

Requiem and Resurrection
4 Hn, 2 Trp, 3 Trb, Tba, 4 Per (14)
C.F. Peters Corp.

Hovhaness, Alan
1911

Tower Music, Op. 129
Fl, Ob, Cl, Bn, 2 Hn, Trp, Trb, Tba (9)
Broude Brothers, Ltd.

Hovland, Egil
1924

Music for Ten Instruments, Op. 28
Fl, Ob, Cl, Bn, Hn, 2 Vn, Va, Vc, Db (10)
Harald Lyche

Höfer, Franz
1880

Sinfonietta, No. 1, Op. 63
2 Vn, Va, Vc, Db, P, Hrm, 2 Fl, Cl, Trp, Hn, Per (13)
C.F. Vieweg Musikverlag

Hrušovský, Ivan
1927

Combinazioni Sonoriche
Fl, Ob, Bcl, Trp, P, Vn, Va, Vc, Per (9)
Slovensky Hudobny Fond

Huggler, John
1928

Music for 13 Instruments, Op. 75
2 Fl, Ob, 2 Cl, Bcl, Bn, Cbn, 2 Hn, Trp, Trb, Vc (13)
C.F. Peters Corp.

Huggler, John
1928

Music, Op. 63
Fl, 2 Cl, 2 Trp, P, Vn, Db, 2 Per (10)
C.F. Peters Corp.

Husa, Karel
1921

Divertimento
2 Hn, 3 Trp, 3 Trb, Tba, 2 Per (11)
Associated Music Publishers

Husa, Karel
1921

Fanfare
4 Hn, 3 Trp, 3 Trb, Tba, Per (12)
Associated Music Publishers

Huse, Peter
1938

Objects
Fl, Ob, Cl, Bn, Hn, Trp, Trb, P, Per (9)
Canadian Music Centre

Hutcheson, Jere
1938

Designs for Fourteen
4 Trp, 2 Hn, 3 Trb, 2 Tba, 3 Per (14)
C.F. Peters Corp.

Hutcheson, Thom
1942

Cañon (Canyon)
Fl, Ob, Bn, Hn, Trp, Trb, Db, Hpd, 2 Per (10)
Middle Tennessee State University

Huybrechts, Lode
1911

Divertissement
4 Trp, 4 Hn, 3 Trb, Tba, Per (13)
Composer's Autograph Publications

Ibert, Jacques
1890-1962

Capriccio
Fl, Ob, Cl, Bn, Trp, Hp, 2 Vn, Va, Vc (10)
Alphonse Leduc

Ippolitov-Ivanov, Mikhail
1859-1935

Caucasian Sketches, Dans la Mosque
2 Fl, Ob, Cl, 2 Bn, 3 Hn, Per (10)
Edwin F. Kalmus

Ishii, Maki
1936

Praeludium und Variationen
Fl, Cl, Bn, Hn, Vn, Va, Vc, P, Per (9)
Ongaku Notomo Sha Corp.

Ives, Charles
1874-1954

Chromatimelotune
Ob, Cl, Bn, Hn, Trp, Trb, Tba, P, 3 Vn, Va, Vc, Db (14)
MJQ Music, Inc.

Ives, Charles
1874-1954

Over the Pavements, Scherzo
Pic, Cl, Bn, Trp, 3 Trb, 2 Per, P (10)
Peer International

Ives, Charles
1874-1954

Symphony No. 3 - The Camp Meeting
Fl, Ob, Cl, Bn, 2 Hn, Trb, Per, 2 Vn, Va, Vc, Db (13)
Associated Music Publishers

Ives, Charles
1874-1954

The Unanswered Question
4 Fl, Trp, 2 Vn, Va, Vc, Db (10)
McGinnis & Marx

Jacob, Gordon
1895-1984

Diversions
Fl, Ob, Cl, Bn, Hn, 2 Vn, Va, Vc, Db (10)
Cambridge Music Shop

Jacob, Gordon
1895-1984

More Old Wine in New Bottles
2 Fl, 2 Ob, 2 Cl, 2 Bn, 2 Hn, Cbn, 2 Trp (13)
June Emerson-Wind Music

Jacob, Gordon
1895-1984

Old Wine in New Bottles
2 Fl, 2 Ob, 2 Cl, 2 Bn, 2 Hn (10)
Oxford University Press

Jacob, Gordon
1895-1984

Salute to U.S.A.
3 Trp, 4 Hn, 3 Trb, Tba, Per (12)
Robert King Music Co.

Jadassohn, Salomon
1831-1902

Serenade, Op. 104
2 Fl, 2 Ob, 2 Cl, 2 Bn, 2 Hn (10)
Andraud

Jadin, Louis
1768-1853

Symphonie
2 Fl, 2 Cl, 3 Bn, 2 Hn, 2 Trp, Trb (12)
Hofmeister Musikverlag

Jaeger, David
1947

Double Woodwind Quintet
2 Fl, 2 Ob, 2 Cl, 2 Bn, 2 Hn (10)
Canadian Music Centre

Janáček, Leoš
1854-1928

Mala Suite
Fl, Ob, Cl, Bn, Hn, Vn, Va, Vc, Db (9)
Ceský Hudební Fond

Jaroch, Jiří
1920

Detska Suita
Fl, Ob, Cl, Bn, Hn, Vn, Va, Vc, Db (9)
Artia

Jaroch, Jiří
1920

Kindersuite
Fl, Ob, Cl, Bn, Hn, Vn, Va, Vc, Db (9)
Artia

Jaroch, Jiří
1920

Nonetto II
Fl, Ob, Cl, Bn, Hn, Vn, Va, Vc, Db (9)
Panton

Jelinek, Hanns
1901-69

Praeludium, Passacaglia and Fugue
Fl, Cl, Bn, Hn, 2 Vn, Va, Vc, Db (9)
Cambridge Music Shop

Jenni, Donald
1937

Allegro
3 Trp, 4 Hn, 3 Trb, Eu, Tba (12)
American Composers Alliance

Jenni, Donald
1937

Allegro
4 Trp, 4 Hn, 3 Trb, Tba, 2Bsx (14)
Composers Facsimile Edition

Jolas, Betsy
1926

J.D.E.
Fl, Ob, Cl, Bn, Hn, Bcl, Trp, Trb, Hp, 2 Vn, Va, Vc, Db (14)
Heugel & Cie

Jolivet, André
1905-74

Fanfares pour Britannicus
4 Trp, 4 Hn, 4 Trb, Tba, Per (14)
Boosey & Hawkes

Jongen, Joseph
1873-1953

Fanfare Héroique, Op. 110
3 Trp, 4 Hn, 3 Trb, Eu, Tba, Per (13)
Centre Belge de Documentation Musicale

Josephs, Wilfred
1927

Concert a Dodici, Op. 21
Fl, Pic, Ob, Eh, Cl, Bcl, Bn, Cbn, Hn, Trp, Trb, Tba (12)
Boosey & Hawkes

Kahn, Erich
1905-56

Actus Tragicus
Fl, Ob, Cl, Bn, Hn, 2 Vn, Va, Vc, Db (10)
American Composers Alliance

Kahn, Erich
1905-56

Petite Suite Bretonne
Fl, Ob, Cl, Bn, Hn, Vn, Va, Vc, Hp (9)
American Composers Alliance

Kahowez, Günter
1940

Bardo-Puls
Fl, Cl, Hn, Trp, Vn, Va, Vc, Db, 2 Per, P (11)
Universal Editions

Kalabis, Viktor
1923

Klasicky Nonet
Fl, Ob, Cl, Bn, Hn, Vn, Va, Vc, Db (9)
Panton

Kanitz, Ernest
1894-1978

Serenade
2 Fl, Ob, 2 Cl, Asx, 2 Bn, Hn, 2 Trp, P, Per (13)
U. of S. Cal.

Kapr, Jan
1914

Omaggio Alla Tromba
2 Trp, 3 Hn, Trb, Tba, Fl, Cl, P, Pic, Cbn, Bcl, Per (14)
Editio Supraphon

Karel, Rudolf
1880-1945

Nonetto
Fl, Ob, Cl, Bn, Hn, Vn, Va, Vc, Db (9)
Ceský Hudební Fond

Karlins, Martin
1932

Concerto Grosso
Fl/Pic, Ob, Cl, Bn, Hn, Trb, Vn, Va, Vc (9)
American Composers Alliance

Kee, Cornelis
1900

Blijde Incomste
2 Trp, 3 Hn, 3 Trb, Tba, Per (10)
Donemus

Kelterborn, Rudolf
1931

Musik
Fl, Ob, 2 Cl, Bn, Hn, Trp, Trb, P (9)
Sirius-Verlag

Ketting, Otto
1935

Intrada Festiva
3 Trp, 4 Hn, 3 Trb, Tba, 2 Per (13)
Stichting Donemus

Ketting, Otto
1935

Variazioni per Orchestra
2 Fl, 2 Ob, 3 Cl, 2 Bn, 2 Hn, 2 Trp, Per, Hp (15)
Stichting Donemus

Keuris, Tristan
1946

Musica Concertante
Cl, Hn, Bn, P, 2 Vn, Va, Vc, Db (9)
Stichting Donemus

Killmayer, Wilhelm
1927

Kindertage
Fl, Va, P, Gt, Eorg, Acc, 5 Per, Zit (11)
B. Schotts' Söhne

Kirchner, Leon
1919

Illuminations
2 Hn, 3 Trp, 4 Trb (9)
Associated Music Publishers

Kirchner, Leon
1919

Music for Twelve
Fl, Ob, Cl, Bn, Hn, Trp, Trb, P, Vn, Va, Vc, Db (12)
Associated Music Publishers

Kirnberger, Johann
1721-83

Twelve Minuets
2 Fl, 2 Ob, 2 Hn, 2 Vn, Hpd (9)
Fétis

Kittl, Johann Friedrich
1806-68

Nonet
Fl, Ob, Cl, 2 Hn, Va, Vc, Db, P (9)
Fétis

Klebanov, Demitri
1907

Ukrainian Concertino
Ob, Cl, Bn, Hn, P, Vn, Va, Vc, Db (9)
Leeds

Kleinsinger, George
1914-82

Design for Woodwinds
2 Fl, 2 Ob, 2 Cl, 2 Bn, Hn (9)
Boston Music Co.

Klingler, Karl
1879-1971

Variations in A Major
Fl, Ob, Cl, Bn, Hn, 2 Vn, Va, Vc, Db (10)
Klingler

Klughardt, August
1847-1902

Nonetto
Fl, Ob, Cl, Bn, 2 Vn, Va, Vc, Db (9)
Fétis

Klusák, Jan
1943

Invention
Fl, Ob, Cl, Bn, Hn, Vn, Va, Vc, Db (9)
Ceský Hudební Fond

Klusák, Jan
1943

Invention for Strings
7 Vn, 2 Va, 2 Vc, Db (12)
Supraphon-Palackeho

Knight, Morris
1933

Varieties for Brass
3 Trp, 4 Hn, 3 Trb, Tba (11)
Studio P/R

Knox, Charles
1929

Symphony
3 Trp, 4 Hn, 3 Trb, Eu, Tba, 2 Per (14)
Musical Evergreen

Knox, Charles
1929

Symphony for Brass & Percussion
3 Trp, 4 Hn, 3 Trb, Eu, Tba, Per (13)
Autograph Editions

Knussen, Oliver
1952

Ophelia Dances I, Op. 13A
Fl, Ob, Cl, Hn, Vn, Va, Vc, P, Cel (9)
Faber Music Ltd.

Knussen, Oliver
1952

Pantomine
Fl, Ob, Cl, Bn, Hn, 2 Vn, Va, Vc (9)
G. Schirmer

Kocscár, Miklós
1933

Capricorn Concerto
Cl, Hn, P, 3 Per, Fl, Vn, Va, Vc (10)
Editio Musica Budapest

Koellreuter, Hans Joachim
1915

Constructio ad Synesin 1962
Pic, Eh, Bcl, Cbn, Vn, Hp, Hpd, P, Per (9)
Edition Modern

Koetsier, Jan
1911

Nonett
Ob, Cl, Bn, Hn, 2 Vn, Va, Vc, Db (9)
Stichting Donemus

Koetsier, Jan
1911

Rondo Sereno
Cl, Bn, Hn, 2 Vn, Va, Vc, Db, P (9)
Stichting Donemus

Kohn, Karl
1926

Impromptus
2 Fl, Cl, 2 Bn, 2 Trp, 2 Trb (9)
Carl Fischer

Kohn, Karl
1926

The Prophet Bird
Fl/Pic, Cl, Bn, Hn, Trb, Vn, Va, Vc, Hp, Per (10)
American Music Center

Kolb, Barbara
1939

Trobar Clus
Fl, Afl, Cl, Bn, Vn, Va, 2 Trp, 2 Trb, Hpd, Per, Gt (13)
Boosey & Hawkes

Kopelent, Marek
1932

A Few Minutes with an Oboist
Ob, Trp, 2 Gt, Man, Ban, Hp, P, 2 Per, Vn, Db (12)
Hans Gerig Musikverlag

Kopelent, Marek
1932

Pocta Vladimiru Holanovi
Fl, Ob, Cl, Bn, Hn, Vn, Va, Vc, Db (9)
Panton

Kornauth, Egon
1891-1959

Chamber Music, Op. 31
Fl, Ob, Cl, Hn, 2 Vn, Va, Vc, Db (9)
Ludwig Doblinger

Kox, Hans
1930

Cyclofonie IV
Rec, 6 Vn, 2 Vc, Db (10)
Stichting Donemus

Kox, Hans
1930

Cyclofony VIII
Fl, Ob, Cl, Bn, Hn, Vn, Va, Vc, Db (9)
Stichting Donemus

Koželuh, Leopold
1747-1818

Two Suites for Wind Nonet
2 Ob, 2 Cl, 2 Hn, 2 Bn, Db (9)
N. Simrock

Krenek, Ernst
1900

Drei Lustige Märsche, Op. 44
Fl, Ob, 4 Cl, 2 Hn, 2 Trp, Trb, Tba, Per (13)
Universal Editions

Krenek, Ernst
1900

Marginal Sounds
Vn, Cel, P, 6 Per (9)
Rongwen Music, Inc.

Krenek, Ernst
1900

Symphonic Music for 9 Solo Inst.
Fl, Ob, Cl, Bn, 2 Vn, Va, Vc, Db (9)
Universal Editions

Krenek, Ernst
1900

Symphony Music Divertimento, Op. 23
Fl, Cl, Bn, Hn, 2 Vn, Va, Vc, Db (9)
Andraud

Krenek, Ernst
1900

Symphony Music in Two Movements, Op. 11
Fl, Ob, Cl, Bn, 2 Vn, Va, Vc, Db (9)
Universal Editions

Kroeger, Karl
1932

The Firebugs Overture and Incidental Music
Cl, Bn, Trp, 2 Trb, Vn, Db, P, Per (9)
Composers Facsimile Edition

Krol, Bernhard
1920

Konzertante Musik, Op. 6
Va, 2 Ob, 2 Cl, 2 Bn, 2 Hn (9)
Breitkopf & Härtel

Krommer, Franz
1759-1831

Armonia in F Major
2 Ob, 2 Cl, 2 Hn, 2 Bn, Cbn (9)
Lorenzi

Krommer, Franz
1759-1831

Concertante, Op. 38 and 39
Fl, Ob, Vn, 2 Va, 2 Hn, Vc, Db (9)
Fétis

Krommer, Franz
1759-1831

Concertino, Op. 18
Fl, Ob, 2 Hn, 3 Vn, Vc, Db (9)
Cambridge Music Shop

Krommer, Franz
1759-1831

Nonet, Op. 79
2 Ob, 2 Cl, 2 Bn, Cbn, 2 Hn (9)
Hofmeister Musikverlag

Kubik, Gail
1914-84

Divertimento No. 1
Fl/Pic, Ob/Eh, Cl/Bcl, Bn, Hn, Trp, Trb, Vn, Va, Vc, Db, Per, P/Hpd (13)
MCA Music

Kubin, Rudolf
1909-73

Nonetto
Fl, Ob, Cl, Bn, Hn, Vn, Va, Vc, Db (9)
Český Hudební Fond

Kubizek, Augustin
1918

Quartetto da Camera, Op. 24a
Fl, Ob, Cl, Bn, Hn, Vn, Va, Vc, Db (9)
Ludwig Doblinger

Kubizek, Augustin
1918

Sinfonia da Camera, Op. 26b
Fl, Ob, Cl, Bn, Hn, Vn, Va, Vc, Db (9)
Ludwig Doblinger

Kučera, Václav
1929

Dramata
Pic, Ob, Cl, Bn, Hn, Vn, Va, Vc, Db (9)
Editio Supraphon

Kupferman, Meyer
1926

Concertino
4 Trp, 2 Hn, 4 Trb, Tba (11)
General Music Publishing Co.

Kupferman, Meyer
1926

Infinites 14
Trp, Pic, 2 Bcl, 2 Per, Vn, Va, Vc, Db, P (11)
General Music Publishing Co.

Kupferman, Meyer
1926

Little Symphony
Fl, 2 Ob, 2 Bn, 2 Hn, 2 Vn, Va, Vc, Db (12)
Eugene Weintraub, Inc.

Kurka, Robert
1921-57

The Good Soldier Schweik Polka and Waltz
Fl, Pic, Ob, Eh, Cl, Bcl, Bn, Cbn, 2 Trp, Trb, Per (15)
Eugene Weintraub, Inc.

Kurtz, Edward
1881-1965

Conversations
Fl, Cl, Bn, Hn, Trp, Trb, Hp, Cel, Gt, Vn, Va, Vc (12)
Jobert & Cie

Kwiatkowski, Ryszard
1931

Baltic Sonnets
Fl, Ob, Cl, Bn, Hn, Vn, Va, Vc, P (9)
Polskie Wydawnictwo Muzyczne

Laderman, Ezra
1924

Cadence
2 Fl, 4 Vn, Va, 2 Vc, Db (10)
G. Schirmer

Laderman, Ezra
1924

Nonette
Fl, Cl, Bn, Trp, Hn, Trb, Vn, Vc, P (9)
Oxford University Press

Lalo, Edouard
1823-92

Morning Serenade
Fl, Ob, Cl, Bn, Hn, 2 Vn, Va, Vc, Db (10)
Heugel & Cie

Lampe, Walther
1872-1964

Serenade, Op. 7
2 Fl, 2 Ob, Eh, 2 Cl, Bcl, 4 Hn, Cbn, 2 Bn (15)
N. Simrock

Lampersberg, Gerhard
1928

Sinfonie
Fl, Cl, Bn, Hn, Trp, Trb, Hp, Cel, Gt, Vn, Va, Vc (12)
Universal Editions

Landré, Guillaume
1905

Sonata Festiva
Fl, Ob, Cl, Bn, Hn, Trp, Per, 2 Vn, Va, Vc, Db (12)
Stichting Donemus

Lange, Gustav
1830-89

Nonet in F Major
2 Ob, Fl, 2 Cl, 2 Hn, 2 Bn (9)
Rud. Erdmann Musik-Verlag

Lanza, Alcides
1929

Eidesis II - 1967 - III
2 Hn, 2 Trb, Tba, 3 Vc, 2 Db, 3 Per (13)
Boosey & Hawkes

Lauber, Joseph
1864-1952

Serenade for 14 Wind Instruments
Fl, Pic, Ob, Eh, 2 Cl, 2 Hn, 2 Bn, 2 Trp, 2 Trb (14)
Manuscript Switzerland

Lazarof, Henri
1932

Espaces
2 Fl, Cl, Bcl, 2 Va, 2 Vc, 2 P (10)
Associated Music Publishers

Lebič, Lojze
1934

Kons (A)
Fl, Cl, Hn, Vn, Va, Vc, P, Hp, Per (9)
DSS Editions

Lebič, Lojze
1934

Kons (b)
3 Cl, 2 Vn, Va, Vc, Hp, Per (9)
DSS Editions

Lebow, Leonard
1929

Suite for Brass
3 Trp, 3 Hn, 3 Trb, Eu, Tba, Per (12)
Summy-Birchard Co.

Lees, Benjamin
1924

Fanfare for a Centennial
3 Trp, 4 Hn, 3 Trb, Tba, Per (12)
Boosey & Hawkes

Legrand, Michel
1932

Porcelaine de Saxe
Trp, Per, Db, 2 Ssx, Asx, Tsx, 2 Bsx (9)
Belwin-Mills Company

Lehmann, Hans
1937

Quanti
Fl, Eh, Bcl/Cl, Bn, Trp, Trb, Hn, Hp, Per, Vn, Va, Vc, Db (13)
Schott & Company, Ltd.

Leibowitz, René
1913

Chamber Concerto, Op. 10
Fl, Ob, Cl, Bn, Hn, Vn, Va, Vc, Db (9)
Universal Editions

Leibowitz, René
1913

Chamber Symphony, Op. 16
Fl, Ob, Cl, Bcl, Bn, Hn, Trp, Trb, Vn, Va, Vc, Db (12)
Boelke-Bomart Publications

Leibowitz, René
1913

Suite, Op. 81
Fl, Ob, Cl, Bn, Hn, Vn, Va, Vc, Db (9)
Jobert & Cie

Leichtling, Alan
1947

Item 72-D
Fl, Ob, 3 Cl, 2 Bn, 2 Hn, 2 Trb, Db (12)
Seesaw Music Corp.

Leitermeyer, Fritz
1925

Divertimento, Op. 53
Pic, Fl, Ob, Eh, Cl, Bcl, Bn, Cbn, 2 Hn, Trp, Trb (12)
Ludwig Doblinger

Leleu, Jeanne
1898-1979

Suite Symphonique
2 Fl, 2 Ob, Cl, Bn, Hn, 2 Trp, Trb, Per, P (12)
Alphonse Leduc

Lendvai, Erno
1925

Kammersuite, Op. 32
Fl, Ob, Cl, Bn, Hn, 2 Vn, Va, Vc, Db, Hp (11)
N. Simrock

Lenot, Jacques
1945

Comme au Loin
2 Fl, 2 Ob, 2 Cl, 2 Bn, 2 Hn (10)
Edizioni Suvini Zerboni

Lessard, John
1920

Concerto for Wind Instruments
2 Fl, Ob, 2 Cl, 2 Bn, 2 Hn, 2 Trp, Trb (12)
Theodore Presser

Levinas, Michael
1949

Strettes Tournantes-Migrations
Fl, Bcl, Bn, 2 Hn, Trp, Va, Vc, Db (9)
Editions Salabert

Lewis, Anthony
1915-83

Pieces of Eight
Fl, 2 Ob, 3 Cl, Bn, Hn, 2 Tsx, Eu, Per (12)
Composer's Autograph Publications

Lewis, John
1920

Milanese Story
Fl, Tsx, Gt, P, Per, 2 Vn, Va, Vc, Db (10)
MJQ Music, Inc.

Lewis, Peter
1932

Lamentation, 3 Epigrams
2 Fl, Ob, Eh, Cl, Bcl, Bn, Cbn, 2 Hn, 2 Vn, Va, Vc (14)
American Composers Alliance

Lewis, Peter
1932

Sestina
2 Fl, 2 Ob, 2 Cl, 2 Bn, Bcl, 2 Hn (11)
American Composers Alliance

Lewis, Robert
1926

Music for Twelve Players
Fl, Cl, Bn, Hn, Trp, Trb, Per, Hp, Vn, Vc, Db, P (12)
Theodore Presser

Liadov, Anatoli
1855-1914

Fanfares
2 Trp, 4 Hn, 3 Trb, Tba, Per (11)
Luck's Music Library

Liber, Anton
1732-1809

Divertimento in Bb Major
2 Cl, 2 Hn, 2 Bn, 2 Va, Db (9)
Manuscript

Lieberson, Peter
1946

Lalita - Chamber Variations
Fl/Pic, Ob, Cl/Bcl, Hn, Per, P, Vn, Va, Vc, Db/P (10)
Associated Music Publishers

Lieberson, Peter
1946

Wind Messengers
3 Fl, 2 Ob, 2 Cl, 2 Bcl, 2 Bn, 2 Hn (13)
Associated Music Publishers

Ligeti, György
1923

Fragment
Cbn, Trb, Tba, Per, Hp, Hpd, P, 3 Db (10)
Universal Editions

Ligeti, György
1923

Kammer Konzert
Fl, Ob, 2 Cl, Hn, Trb, Cem/Hrm, P, Cel, 2 Vn, Va, Vc, Db (14)
Schott & Company, Ltd.

Lilien, Ignace
1897-1964

Sonatine Apollinique
2 Fl, 2 Ob, 2 Cl, 2 Bn, 2 Hn (10)
Stichting Donemus

Linke, Norbert
1933

Profit Tout Clair
Ob, Cl, Bn, Hn, 2 Vn, Va, Vc, Db (9)
Hans Gerig Musikverlag

Linn, Robert
1925

Concertino
Vn, 2 Fl, 2 Ob, 2 Cl, 2 Bn (9)
Western International Music

Loeb, David
1939

Partita da Camera
Fl, Ob., Cl, Bn, 3 Vn, Va, Vc, Db (10)
Branch

Lombardi, Luca
1945

Gespräch über Bäume
Fl, Cl, Vn, Va, Vc, Trb, P, 2 Per (9)
Hermann Moeck Verlag

Lorentzen, Bent
1935

Wunderblumen
Fl, Ob, Cl, Bn, P, 2 Vn, Va, Vc, Db (10)
Wilhelm Hansen Musik-Forlag

Louel, Jean
1914

Fanfare J.M.
3 Trp, 4 Hn, 3 Trb, Tba, Per (12)
Centre Belge de Documentation Musicale

Louel, Jean
1914

Fanfares
3 Trp, 4 Hn, 3 Trb, Tba, Per (12)
Centre Belge de Documentation Musicale

Louis Ferdinand, Prince of Prussia
1772-1806

Rondo, Op. 9
2 Vn, Va, Vc, Db, Fl, Cl, 2 Hn, P (10)
Boosey & Hawkes

Luening, Otto
1900

Fanfare for a Festive Occasion
3 Trp, 3 Hn, 3 Trb, Per (10)
C.F. Peters Corp.

Luigini, Alexandre
1850-1906

Aubade, Op. 13
3 Fl, Ob, 2 Cl, Bn, Hn, Hp (9)
Andraud

Lutoslawski, Witold
1913

Dance Preludes
2 Vn, Va, Vc, Db, 2 Vn, Va, Vc (9)
Chester Music Limited

Lutoslawski, Witold
1913

Slides
Fl, Ob, Cl, Bn, Hn, Per, P/Cel, Vn, Va, Vc, Db (11)
Chester Music Limited

Lutyens, Elizabeth
1906

Chamber Concerto No. 1
Ob, Cl, Bn, Hn, Trp, Trb, Vn, Va, Vc (9)
J. & W. Chester Ltd.

Lutyens, Elizabeth
1906

Music for Wind
2 Fl, 2 Ob, 2 Cl, 2 Bn, 2 Hn (10)
Schott & Company, Ltd.

Lutyens, Elizabeth
1906

Six Tempi
Fl, Ob, Cl, Bn, Hn, Trp, Vn, Va, Vc, P (10)
Belwin-Mills Company

Lybbert, Donald
1923-81

Sonorities
Pic, Fl, 2 Cl, 2 Asx, Hn, Vn, Va, Vc, P (11)
American Composers Alliance

Macchi, Egisto
1928

Composizione 3
Fl, Ob, Cl, Bn, Hn, Trp, Trb, Vn, 2 Va, Vc, Db (12)
Aldo Bruzzichelli

Maderna, Bruno
1920

Serenata No. 2
Fl, Cl, Bcl, Hn, Trp, Vn, Va, Db, P, Per, Hp (11)
Edizioni Suvini Zerboni

Maes, Jef
1905

De Verloofden
Fl, Ob, Cl, Bn, 3 Vn, Va, Vc, Db, P, Per (12)
CeBeDem

Maganini, Quinto
1897-1974

Shenandoah
3 Trp, 2 Hn, 3 Trb, Eu, Tba (10)
Edition Musicus, Inc.

Mailman, Martin
1932

Two Fanfares, Op. 49
3 Trp, 3 Hn, 3 Trb (9)
Southern Music Co.

Maksymiuk, Jerzy
1936

Decet
Fl, Ob, Cl, Bn, Hn, P, 2 Vn, Va, Vc (10)
Polskie Wydawnictwo Muzyczne

Malipiero, Gian
1882-1973

Serenata Mattutina
Fl, Ob, Cl, 2 Bn, 2 Hn, Cel, 2 Va (10)
Universal Editions

Malipiero, Riccardo
1914

Mosaico
Fl, Ob, Cl, Bn, Hn, 2 Vn, Va, Vc, Db (10)
Edizioni Suvini Zerboni

Malipiero, Riccardo
1914

Ricercari
Fl/Pic, Ob, Cl, Bn, Hn, 4 Va, Vc, Db (11)
C.F. Peters Corp.

Manzoni, Giacomo
1932

Parafrasi Con Finale
Fl, Cl, Bn, Hn, Trp, Trb, Hpd, Org, Db, Per (10)
Edizioni Suvini Zerboni

Manzoni, Giacomo
1932

Spiel per 10
6 Vn, 2 Va, 2 Vc, Db (10)
Edizioni Suvini Zerboni

Marcus, Ada Belle Gross
1928

A Setting to Seasons
Fl, Ob, Cl, 2 Vn, Va, Vc, Db, P (9)
Ada Belle Gross Marcus

Maros, Rudolf
1917

Musica da Camera
Fl, 2 Cl, 2 Vn, Va, Vc, Db, Hpd, Per, Hp (11)
Southern Music Pub. Co., Inc.

Marteau, Henri
1874-1934

Sérénade, Op. 20
2 Fl, 2 Ob, 2 Cl, Bcl, 2 Bn (9)
Steingraber-Verlag

Martinů, Bohuslav
1890-1959

Nonetto
Fl, Ob, Cl, Bn, Hn, Vn, Va, Vc, Db (9)
Artia

Martinů, Bohuslav
1890-1959

Pastorals
5 Rec, Cl, 2 Vn, Vc (9)
Bärenreiter & Neuwerk

Martinů, Bohuslav
1890-1959

Serenade No. 4, Divertimento
2 Ob, 3 Vn, 2 Va, Vc, Db, P (10)
Artia

Marttinen, Tauno
1912

Nonet
Fl, Ob, Cl, Bn, Hn, Vn, Va, Vc, Db (9)
Finnish Music Information Centre

Mason, Benedict
1954

Imposing a Regular Pattern in Chaos and Heterophony
Fl, Ob, Cl, Trp, Per, P, 2 Vn, Va, Vc, Db (11)
Chester Music Limited

Mason, Benedict
1954

The Hinterstoisser Traverse
Fl, Ob, Cl, Bn, Hn, Trp, Trb, Per, P, Vn, Va, Vc (12)
Chester Music Limited

Massenet, Jules
1842-1912

Introduction & Variations, Op. 19
Fl, Ob, Cl, Bn, 2 Vn, Va, Vc, Db (9)
Fétis

Masson, Gérard
1936

Quest I
Fl, Trp, Trb, Cl, Bcl, Bn, P, Hp, Vn, Vc (10)
Editions Salabert

Maštalíř, Jaroslav
1906

Nonetto
Fl, Ob, Cl, Bn, Hn, Vn, Va, Vc, Db (9)
Ceský Hudební Fond

Matsudaira, Yoritsune
1907

Serenata
Fl, Ob, Cl, 6 Vn, Per (10)
Edizioni Suvini Zerboni

Matsushita, Shin-Ichi
1922

5 Tempos for 11 Instruments
Fl, Cl, Trp, Trb, Per, P, Va, Vc, Db (11)
Ongaku Notomo Sha Corp.

Matsushita, Shin-Ichi
1922

Correlations for 3 Groups
Fl, Pic, Cl, Asx, Bcl, Vn, Va, Vc, Db, P, Cel, Per (12)
Ongaku Notomo Sha Corp.

Matthews, Colin
1946

Ceres
3 Fl, 2 Vc, Db, Gt, 2 Per (9)
Faber Music Ltd.

Matthews, William
1950

Letters from Home
Fl/Pic, Cl, Bn, Va, Db, P, Hpd, 4 Per (11)
American Composers Alliance

Mayer, William
1925

Essay for Brass and Winds
Fl, Ob, Cl, Bn, 2 Hn, 2 Trp, Trb, Tba, Per (11)
Boosey & Hawkes

Mazzinghi, Joseph
1765-1844

Some Pieces in Harmony, Op. 33
4 Cl, 2 Pic, 2 Bn, 2 Hn, Trp, Ser, Trb (13)
Fétis

McBeth, William Francis
1933

Canticle
4 Hn, 3 Trb, Eu, Tba, 2 Fl, Per (12)
Southern Music Co.

McCauley, William
1917

Five Miniatures
Fl, Ob, Cl, Bn, 2 Hn, 2 Trp, Trb, Tba (10)
Canadian Music Centre

McKay, George Frederick
1899-1970

Bravura Prelude
4 Trp, 4 Hn, 4 Trb, 2 Eu, Tba (15)
Associated Music Publishers

Méfano, Paul
1937

Interferences
Fl, Ob, Cl, Bn, Hn, Vn, Va, Vc, P, Per (10)
Heugel & Cie

Melin, Bengt
1928

Menuet Badin
2 Fl, 2 Ob, 2 Cl, 2 Bn, 2 Hn (10)
Andraud

Merikanto, Aarre
1893-1958

Nonetto
Fl, Eh, Cl, P, 2 Vn, Va, Vc, Db (9)
Musiikin Tiedotuskeskus

Meriläinen, Usko
1930

Impression
Fl, Ob, Cl, Bn, Hn, Va, Vc, Db, P, Per (10)
Bote & Bock

Meriläinen, Usko
1930

Partiti
4 Trp, 4 Hn, 3 Trb, Tba (12)
Robert King Music Co.

Meulemans, Arthur
1884

Fanfare voor de Inauguratie van K.V.S.
3 Trp, 4 Hn, 3 Trb, Tba, Per (12)
Centre Belge de Documentation Musicale

Meyerowitz, Jan
1913

Short Suite
3 Trp, 3 Hn, 2 Trb, Tba (9)
Rongwen Music, Inc.

Mica, Frantisek Adam
1746-1811

Concertino Notturno
3 Vn, 2 Ob, 2 Hn, 2 Bn, 2 Va, Db (12)
Boosey & Hawkes

Michel, Joseph
1708-70

Serenata
2 Fl, 2 Ob, Bn, 2 Hn, 2 Vn, Va, Db (11)
Breitkopf & Härtel

Michel, Joseph
1708-70

Serenata
2 Hn, 2 Ob, 2 Fl, Bn, 2 Vn, Db (10)
Breitkopf & Härtel

Miereanu, Costin
1943

Couleurs du Temps
4 Vn, 2 Va, 2 Vc, Db (9)
Editions Salabert

Mikoda, Bořivoj
1904-70

Nonetto, Op. 30
Fl, Ob, Cl, Bn, Hn, Vn, Va, Vc, Db (9)
Cesky Hudebni Fond

Milhaud, Darius
1892-1974

Actualités
2 Cl, 2 Trp, Trb, Per, 2 Vn, 2 Va, 2 Vc, Db (13)
Universal Editions

Milhaud, Darius
1892-1974

Aspen Serenade
Fl, Ob, Cl, Bn, Trp, Vn, Va, Vc, Db (9)
Heugel & Cie

Milhaud, Darius
1892-1974

Concertino d'Automne
Fl, Ob, 3 Hn, 2 Va, Vc, 2 P (10)
Heugel & Cie

Milhaud, Darius
1892-1974

Dixtuor à cordes
4 Vn, 2 Va, 2 Vc, 2 Db (10)
Universal Editions

Milhaud, Darius
1892-1974

Musique pour Graz
Fl, Ob, Cl, Bn, Hn, Vn, Va, Vc, Db (9)
Universal Editions

Milhaud, Darius
1892-1974

Printemps
Pic, Fl, Ob, Cl, 2 Vn, Va, Vc, Hp (9)
Universal Editions

Mills, Charles
1914

Chamber Concerto
Fl, Ob, Cl, Bn, 2 Hn, 2 Vn, Va, Vc (10)
American Composers Alliance

Mingus, Charles
1922-79

Revelations
Fl, Asx, Tsx, Hn, Trp, Trb, Bn, Hp, P, Gt, Db, 2 Per (13)
Margun Music, Inc.

Miroglio, Francis
1924

Espaces V
Fl, Ob, Cl, Bn, 2 Vn, Va, Vc, Db (9)
Edizioni Suvini Zerboni

Miroglio, Francis
1924

Réseaux
Fl, Cl, Bn, Trb, 2 Vn, Va, Vc, Hp, Per (10)
Universal Editions

Mitrea-Celarianu, Mihai
1935

Signaux
Pic, Fl, Cl, Bcl, Trp, Trb, Tba, P, Vn, Va, Db, 2 Per (13)
Editions Salabert

Molbe, Heinrich 1835-1915	Dezett, Op. 21 Cl, Eh, Bn, Hn, 3 Vn, Va, Vc, Db (10) Hofmeister Musikverlag
Molbe, Heinrich 1835-1915	Dezett, Op. 91 Cl, Eh, Hn, Bn, Hp, 2 Vn, Va, Vc, Db (10) Hofmeister Musikverlag
Molbe, Heinrich 1835-1915	Dezett, Op. 104 Cl, Eh, Hn, Bn, Hp, 2 Vn, Va, Vc, Db (10) Hofmeister Musikverlag
Molbe, Heinrich 1835-1915	Dezett, Op. 109 Cl, Eh, H, Bn, Hp, 2 Vn, Va, Vc, Db (10) Hofmeister Musikverlag
Molbe, Heinrich 1835-1915	Dezett, Op. 113 Cl, Eh, Hn, Bn, Hp, 2 Vn, Va, Vc, Db (10) Hofmeister Musikverlag
Molbe, Heinrich 1835-1915	Dezett, Op. 118 Cl, Eh, Hn, Bn, Hp, 2 Vn, Va, Vc, Db (10) Hofmeister Musikverlag
Molbe, Heinrich 1835-1915	Dezett, Op. 124 Cl, Eh, Hn, Bn, Hp, 2 Vn, Va, Vc, Db (10) Hofmeister Musikverlag
Molbe, Heinrich 1835-1915	Dezett, Op. 129 Cl, Eh, Hn, Bn, Hp, 2 Vn, Va, Vc, Db (10) Hofmeister Musikverlag
Molbe, Heinrich 1835-1915	Grüne Klänge, Op. 141 Cl, Eh, Hn, Bn, Hp, 2 Vn, Va, Vc, Db (10) Hofmeister Musikverlag
Molbe, Heinrich 1835-1915	Hymn De Printemps, Op. 31 Cl, Eh, Hn, Bn, Hp, 2 Vn, Va, Vc, Db (10) Hofmeister Musikverlag
Molbe, Heinrich 1835-1915	Intermezzo, Op. 81 Ob, Cl, Hn, Bn, 2 Vn, Va, Vc, Db (9) Hofmeister Musikverlag
Molbe, Heinrich 1835-1915	Intermezzo, Op. 110 Cl, Eh, Hn, Bn, Hp, 2 Vn, Va, Vc, Db (10) Hofmeister Musikverlag
Molbe, Heinrich 1835-1915	Intermezzo, Op. 111 Cl, Eh, Hn, Bn, Hp, 2 Vn, Va, Vc, Db (10) Hofmeister Musikverlag

Molbe, Heinrich
1835-1915

Nonet, Op. 26
Ob, Cl, Hn, Bn, 2 Vn, Va, Vc, Db (9)
Hofmeister Musikverlag

Molbe, Heinrich
1835-1915

Nonet, Op. 61
Cl, Eh, Hn, Bn, 2 Vn, Va, Vc, Db (9)
Hofmeister Musikverlag

Molbe, Heinrich
1835-1915

Nonet, Op. 83
Ob, Cl, Hn, Bn, 2 Vn, Va, Vc, Db (9)
Hofmeister Musikverlag

Molbe, Heinrich
1835-1915

Nonet, Op. 84
Ob, Cl, Hn, Bn, 2 Vn, Va, Vc, Db (9)
Hofmeister Musikverlag

Molbe, Heinrich
1835-1915

Nonet, Op. 89
Ob, Cl, Hn, Bn, 2 Vn, Va, Vc, Db (9)
Hofmeister Musikverlag

Montsalvatge, Bassols Xavier
1912

5 Invocaciones al Crucificado
Fl, 2 Ob, 2 Cl, Bn, 2 Hn, Trp, Per, Cel, Hp, P, Db (14)
Union Musical Española

Moór, Emanuel
1863-1931

Dixtuor, Op. 103
Fl, Ob, Cl, Bn, Hn, 2 Vn, Va, Vc, Db (10)
Andraud

Moór, Emanuel
1863-1931

Suite, Op. 103
Fl, Ob, Cl, Bn, Hn, 2 Vn, Va, Vc, Db (10)
Editions Salabert

Morawetz, Lucien
1901-73

Sinfonietta
3 Trp, 4 Hn, 2 Fl, 2 Cl, Bn, Per (13)
Leeds

Mortari, Virgilio
1902

Fantasia Concertante per 12
6 Vn, 3 Va, 2 Vc, Db (12)
Edizioni Suvini Zerboni

Morthenson, Jan W.
1941

Antiphonia
3 Fl, 2 Cl, 3 Vn, 3 Va, Vc, Db (13)
Wilhelm Hansen Musik-Forlag

Morthenson, Jan W.
1941

Antiphonia III
Fl, Cl, Bn, Hn, Trb, Org, Per, Vn, Va, Vc, Db (11)
Nordiska Musikforlaget

Moser, Franz
1880-1939

Serenade, Op. 35
2 Fl, 3 Ob, 3 Cl, 3 Bn, 4 Hn (15)
Universal Editions

Moulaert, Raymond
1875-1962

Fanfares
3 Trp, 4 Hn, 3 Trb, Tba, 2 Bn, Per (14)
Centre Belge de Documentation Musicale

Moyse, Louis
1912

Divertimento
2 Fl, 2 Ob, 2 Cl, 2 Bn, 2 Hn, 2 Vc, Db, Per (14)
McGinnis & Marx

Mozart, Wolfgang Amadeus
1756-91

Cassazione, K. 63
2 Ob, 2 Hn, 2 Vn, Va, Vc, Db (9)
Boosey & Hawkes

Mozart, Wolfgang Amadeus
1756-91

Cassazione, K. 99
2 Ob, 2 Hn, 2 Vn, Va, Vc, Db (9)
Boosey & Hawkes

Mozart, Wolfgang Amadeus
1756-91

Divertimento, K. 113
2 Cl, 2 Hn, 2 Vn, Va, Vc, Db (9)
Boosey & Hawkes

Mozart, Wolfgang Amadeus
1756-91

Divertimento, K. 131
2 Vn, 2 Va, Vc, Db, Fl, Ob, Vn, 4 Hn (13)
Boosey & Hawkes

Mozart, Wolfgang Amadeus
1756-91

Divertimento, K. 166
2 Ob, 2 Cl, 2 Eh, 2 Hn, 2 Bn (10)
Boosey & Hawkes

Mozart, Wolfgang Amadeus
1756-91

Divertimento, K. 186
2 Ob, 2 Cl, 2 Eh, 2 Hn, 2 Bn (10)
Boosey & Hawkes

Mozart, Wolfgang Amadeus
1756-91

Divertimento, K. 187
2 Fl, 5 Trp, 4 Per (11)
Boosey & Hawkes

Mozart, Wolfgang Amadeus
1756-91

Divertimento, K. 188
2 Fl, 5 Trp, 4 Per (11)
Boosey & Hawkes

Mozart, Wolfgang Amadeus
1756-91

Galimathias Musicum, K. 32
2 Ob, 2 Hn, Bn, 2 Vn, Va, Vc, Hpd (10)
C.F. Peters Corp.

Mozart, Wolfgang Amadeus
1756-91

Masonic Funeral Music, K. 477
2 Ob, Cl, Cbn, 2 Hn, Bhn, 2 Vn, Va, Vc, Db (12)
Edizioni Suvini Zerboni

Mozart, Wolfgang Amadeus
1756-91

Serenade, K. 100
2 Ob(2 Fl), 2 Hn, 2 Trp, 2 Vn, Va, Db (10)
Andraud

Mozart, Wolfgang Amadeus 1756-91	Serenade, K. 320 2 Fl, 2 Ob, 2 Bn, 2 Hn, 2 Trp, Per, 2 Vn, Va, Db (15) Andraud
Mozart, Wolfgang Amadeus 1756-91	Serenade, K. 361 2 Ob, 2 Cl, 2 Bhn(2 Cl), 2 Bn, Cbn(Db), 4 Hn (13) Broude Brothers, Ltd.
Mulder, Ernest 1898	Fuga No. 4 Fl, Ob, Cl, Hn, 2 Vn, Va, Vc, Db (9) Stichting Donemus
Müller-Zürich, Paul 1898	Marienleben, Op. 8 Acht Stücke Fl, Ob, Cl, Hn, 2 Vn, Va, Vc, Db (9) B. Schotts' Söhne
Musgrave, Thea 1928	Chamber Concerto No. 1 Ob, Cl, Bn, Hn, Trp, Trb, Vn, Va, Vc (9) J. & W. Chester Ltd.
Nagel, Robert 1924	Divertimento Fl, Ob, Cl, Bn, 2 Hn, 2 Trp, Trb, Tba (10) Mentor Music, Inc.
Napoli, Carlo 1939	Appunti per Don Chisciotte Fl, Cl, Bn, Hn, Trp, Tp, Per, P, 2 Vn, Va, Vc, Db (13) Casa Musicale Sonzogno
Naumann, Ernst 1832-1910	Serenade, Op. 10 Fl, Ob, Bn, Hn, 2 Vn, Va, Vc, Db (9) N. Simrock
Naumann, Robert 1844-1906	Kammermusik, Op. 31 Fl, Ob, Cl, Hn, 2 Vn, Va, Vc, Db (9) Ludwig Doblinger
Naumann, Siegfried 1919	Cadenze Cl, Vn, Vc, 2 Trp, Hn, Trb, Fl, Per (9) STIMS Informationscentral för Svensk Musik
Nelhybel, Vaclav 1919	Ancient Hungarian Dances 3 Trp, 2 Hn, 3 Trb, 2 Eu, Tba (11) Franco Colombo, Inc.
Nelhybel, Vaclav 1919	Chorale 3 Trp, 2 Hn, 3 Trb, Eu, Tba (10) General Music Publishing Co.
Nelhybel, Vaclav 1919	Concerto Antifonale 4 Trp, 3 Hn, 5 Trb, 2 Tba (14) Franco Colombo, Inc.

Nelhybel, Vaclav
1919

Designs for Brass
3 Trp, 4 Hn, 3 Trb, Eu, Tba (12)
Boosey & Hawkes

Nelhybel, Vaclav
1919

Motet & Pavane
2 Trp, 3 Hn, 3 Trb, Tba, 2 Per (11)
Belwin-Mills Company

Nelhybel, Vaclav
1919

Motet and Pavane
3 Trp, 2 Hn, 2 Trb, 2 Eu, Tba (10)
Franco Colombo, Inc.

Nelhybel, Vaclav
1919

Slavic March
3 Trp, 3 Hn, 3 Trb, Eu, Tba, Per (12)
General Music Publishing Co.

Nelhybel, Vaclav
1919

Three Intradas for Brass Choir
3 Trp, 2 Hn, 3 Trb, Tba (9)
General Music Publishing Co.

Niblock, James
1917

Triptych for Brass
3 Trp, 4 Hn, 3 Trb, Eu, Tba, Per (13)
Crescendo Music Sales Co.

Nielsen, Riccardo
1908

Fasce Sonore (6+5)
6 Vn, 2 Va, 2 Vc, Db (11)
G. Ricordi & Co.

Nikodemowicz, Andrzej
1925

Chamber Concerto
Fl, Cl, Bn, Hn, Vn, Db, P, 4 Per (11)
Polskie Wydawnictwo Muzyczne

Nilsson, Bo
1937

Frequenzen
Pic, Fl, 4 Per, Org, Gt, Db (9)
Universal Editions

Nilsson, Bo
1937

Zeitpunkte
Fl, Afl, Ob, Eh, Cl, Bcl, Asx, Tsx, Bn, Cbn (10)
Universal Editions

Nono, Luigi
1924-90

Canti per 13
Fl, Ob, 2 Cl, Tsx, Bn, Hn, Trp, Trb, Vn, Va, Vc, Db (13)
Schott & Company, Ltd.

Nordenstrom, Gladys
1924

El-Greco-Fantasie
8 Vn, Va, Vc, Db (11)
Bärenreiter Verlag

Novák, Jan
1921-84

Baletti a 9
Fl, Ob, Cl, Bn, Hn, Vn, Va, Vc, Db (9)
Artia

Novy, Donald
1932

Sonatina
3 Trp, 3 Hn, 3 Trb, Per (10)
Robert King Music Co.

Nunes, Emanuel
1941

Dawn Wo
2 Fl, Ob, Eh, 3 Cl, Bn, Cbn, 2 Hn, Trp, Trb (13)
Jobert & Cie

Nunes, Emanuel
1941

Omens
Fl, Cl, Trp, Trb, Va, Vc, Hp, Per, Cel (9)
Jobert & Cie

Nystedt, Knut
1915

Pia Memoria
2 Trp, 2 Hn, 3 Trb, Tba, 2 Per (10)
Associated Music Publishers

Odstrčil, Karel
1930

Siluety
Fl, Ob, Cl, Bn, Hn, Vn, Va, Vc, Db (9)
Panton

Olah, Tiberiu
1928

Perspectives
Fl, Ob/Eh, Cl/Bcl, Hn, Trp, Trb, Vn, Va, Vc, Db, 3 Per (13)
Editions Salabert

Olan, David
1948

Gathering
Fl/Pic, Cl/Bcl, Trp, Trb, Vn, Vc, P, 2 Per (9)
American Composers Alliance

Olan, David
1948

Music
Fl, Cl, Bn, Hn, Trp, Trb, Vn, Va, Vc, 4 Per (13)
American Composers Alliance

Onslow, George
1784-1852

Nonetto, Op. 77
Fl, Ob, Cl, Bn, Hn, Vn, Va, Vc, Db (9)
McGinnis & Marx

Ordoñez, Carlos d'
1734-86

Five Chamber Symphonies
2 Vn, Va, Vc, 2 Ob, 2 Hn, 2 Trp, Per (11)
Manuscript Brussels

Osterc, Slavko
1895-1941

Nonet
Fl, Ob, Cl, Bn, Hn, Vn, Va, Vc, Db (9)
DSS Editions

Otten, Ludwig
1924

Divertimento
Fl, 2 Ob, 2 Cl, 2 Bn, 2 Hn (9)
Stichting Donemus

Otterloo, Willem van
1907-78

Intrada
4 Trp, 4 Hn, 4 Trb, Tba, Vn, Per (15)
Stichting Donemus

Overton, Hall
1920-72

Pulsations
Fl, Cl, Bn, Hn, Trp, Trb, Vn, Vc, Db, P, Hp, Per (12)
American Composers Alliance

Pablo, Luis de
1930

Credo
2 Fl, 2 Ob, 2 Cl, 2 Bn, 2 Hn (10)
Edizioni Suvini Zerboni

Pablo, Luis de
1930

Modulos I
3 Cl, 2 Vn, Va, Vc, 2 P, 2 Per (11)
Edition Tonos

Paccagnini, Angelo
1930

Musica da Camera
Pic, Fl, Bcl, Hn, Vn, Vc, Db, Hp, Per (9)
Universal Editions

Pálsson, Páll
1928

Crystals
Fl, Ob, Cl, Bn, Hn, 2 Vn, Va, Vc (9)
Islenzk

Parchman, Gene
1929

Fifth Symphony
6 Per, Tp, Db, P (9)
Seesaw Music Corp.

Parodi, Renato
1900

Concerto
Fl, 4 Vn, 2 Va, 2 Vc, 2 Db, Hp, Cel (13)
G. Ricordi & Co.

Parris, Herman
1903

Four Rhapsodies
3 Trp, 4 Hn, 3 Trb, Tba (11)
Elkan-Vogel

Parris, Robert
1924

Lamentations & Praises
3 Trp, 2 Hn, 3 Trb, Tba (39)
C.F. Peters Corp.

Parris, Robert
1924

The Golden Net
Fl, Ob, Cl, Bn, Hn, Trp, Vn, Va, Vc, 2 Per (11)
American Composers Alliance

Parry, Charles Hubert
1848-1918

Nonet, Op. 70
Fl, Ob, Eh, 2 Cl, 2 Hn, 2 Bn (9)
June Emerson-Wind Music

Pauer, Ernst
1826-1905

Divertimento
Fl, Ob, Cl, Bn, Hn, Vn, Va, Vc, Db (9)
Cambridge Music Shop

Pauer, Jiří
1919

Musica da Concerto
2 Fl, 2 Ob, 2 Cl, 2 Bn, 2 Hn, 2 Trp, Trb (13)
Artia

Paumgartner, Bernhard
1887-1971

Divertimento
Pic, Eh, Asx, Bn, Hn, Trp, P, Va, Vc, Per (10)
Universal Editions

Payne, Anthony
1936

Fanfares and Processional
Hn, 4 Trp, 4 Trb, Tba (10)
Chester Music Limited

Peaslee, Richard
1930

Divertimento
2 Trp, 3 Hn, 3 Trb, Tba, Per (10)
Joseph Boonin, Incorp.

Penderecki, Krzysztof
1933

Capriccio
Ob, 6 Vn, 2 Va, 2 Vc, Db (12)
Hermann Moeck Verlag

Perilhou, Albert
1846-1936

Divertissement
2 Fl, 2 Ob, 2 Cl, 2 Bn, 4 Hn (12)
Andraud

Persichetti, Vincent
1915-87

Serenade No. 1
Fl, Ob, Cl, Bn, Hn, 2 Trp, Hn, Trb, Tba (10)
Elkan-Vogel

Peterson, Wayne
1927

Encounters
Fl/Pic, Cl/Bcl, Hn, Trp, Vn, Vc, P, 2 Per (9)
American Music Center

Petrescu, Dinu
1939

Musique
Fl, Cl, Trp, Vn, Va, Vc, Db, P, Hp, Org, Hpd, Per (12)
Editions Salabert

Petrić, Ivo
1931

Divertimento for Slavko Osterc
Fl, Ob, Cl, Bn, Hn, P, Hp, Per, 2 Vn, Va, Vc, Db (13)
Edicije Društva Slovenskih Skladateljev

Petrić, Ivo
1931

Inlaid-Work
Fl, Cl, Trp, Vn, Va, Vc, Db, Per (12)
Edicije Društva Slovenskih Skladateljev

Petrić, Ivo
1931

Petit Concerto De Chambre
Ob, Cl, Bcl, Hn, Vn, Va, Vc, Db, Hp (9)
Edicije Društva Slovenskih Skladateljev

Petyrek, Felix
1892-1951

Arabische Suite
2 Fl, Ob, 2 Cl, 2 Bn, 2 Hn, Trb, Hp, Db, Per (13)
Universal Editions

Phillips, Peter
1930

Chimer
Fl/Pic, Cl, Eh, Cbn, Hn, Vn, Va, Vc, Db, Trp/Fn, Trb, Tba (12)
MJQ Music Inc.

Piechowska, Alina
1937

Imaginaire
Ob, 7 Vn, 2 Va, 2 Vc, Db (13)
Polskie Wydawnictwo Muzyczne

Pierné, Gabriel
1863-1937

March of Little Fauns
Fl, Ob, Cl, Bn, Hn, 2 Vn, Va, Vc, Db (10)
Andraud

Pierné, Gabriel
1863-1937

March of the Little Lead Soldiers
Fl, Cl, Trp, Per, Hp, Vn, Va, Vc, Db (9)
Andraud

Pisk, Paul
1893

Cortège, Op. 53B
3 Trp, 2 Hn, 3 Trb, Eu, Tba, 3 Cor (13)
American Composers Alliance

Piston, Walter
1894-1976

Ceremonial Fanfare
4 Trp, 6 Hn, 3 Trb, Tba, Per (15)
Associated Music Publishers

Piston, Walter
1894-1976

Divertimento for Nine Inst.
Fl, Ob, Cl, Bn, 2 Vn, Va, Vc, Db (9)
Associated Music Publishers

Piston, Walter
1894-1976

Fanfare
3 Trp, 4 Hn, 3 Trb, Tba, 4 Per (15)
Boosey & Hawkes

Pittaluga, Gustavo
1906

Petite Suite
Fl, Cl, Bn, Trp, Trb, Hp, 2 Vn, Va, Vc (10)
Spratt

Pleskow, Raoul
1931

Movement for 9 Players
Fl, Cl, Vn, Vc, Trp, Db, P, Per, Cel (9)
McGinnis & Marx

Polin, Claire
1926

The Journey of Owain Madoc
2 Trp, Hn, Trb, Tba, 10 Per (15)
Seesaw Music Corp.

Pollock, Robert
1946

Revolution
Fl, Cl, Bn, Vn, Db, Gt, 2 Per (9)
Boelke-Bomart Publications Ponse, Luctor

Ponse, Luctor
1914

Euterpe, Op. 37
2 Fl, 2 Ob, 3 Cl, 2 Bn, 2 Hn (11)
Stichting Donemus

Pospíšil, Jurraj
1931

Nonet No. 2
Fl, Ob, Bcl, Trp, Hn, Vn, Va, Vc, P, Per (9)
Slovensky Hudobny Fond

Pospíšil, Jurraj
1931

Trojversia, Op. 22
Fl, Bcl, Hn, Trp, Trb, Per, Vn, Va, Vc (9)
Slovensky Hudobny Fond

Post, Jennifer
1949

The Next Call
Fl, Ob, Cl, Bn, 2 Hn, Trp, Trb, 2 Db (10)
Stichting Donemus

Poulenc, Francis
1899-1963

Mouvements Perpétuels
Fl, Ob, Cl, Bn, Hn, Vn, Va, Vc, Db (9)
Chester Music Limited

Poulenc, Francis
1899-1963

Suite Française
2 Trp, 3 Trb, 2 Ob, 2 Bn, Per (10)
Durand et Cie

Powell, Mel
1923

Modules
Fl, Ob, Cl, Bn, 2 Hn, Trp, Trb, 2 Per, Vn, Va, Vc, Db (14)
Wilhelm Hansen Musik-Forlag

Praag, Henri C. Van
1894-1968

Dixtuor
Fl, Ob, Cl, Bn, Hn, 2 Vn, Va, Vc, Db (10)
Stichting Donemus

Praag, Henri C. Van
1894-1968

Fantasie
2 Fl, 2 Ob, 2 Cl, 2 Hn, Bn (9)
Stichting Donemus

Pragg, Henri C. Van
1894-1968

Music
2 Fl, 2 Ob, 3 Cl, 2 Bn, 2 Hn (11)
Stichting Donemus

Pratella, Francesco
1880-1955

Per un Dramma Orientale, Op. 40
Fl, Ob, Cl, Bn, Hn, 2 Vn, Va, Vc, Db (10)
G. Ricordi & Co.

Premru, Raymond
1934

Divertimento for Brass
Hn, 4 Trp, 4 Trb, Tba (10)
Chester Music Limited

Presser, William
1916

Passacaglia and Fugue
3 Trp, 4 Hn, 3 Trb, Eu, Tba, 2 Per (14)
Tenuto Publications

Presser, William
1916

Research
3 Trp, 3 Hn, 3 Trb, 2 Eu, Tba (12)
Tenuto Publications

Raff, Joseph Joachim
1822-82

Sinfonietta, Op. 188
2 Fl, 2 Ob, 2 Cl, 2 Bn, 2 Hn (10)
Andraud

Ramovš, Primož
1921

Apel
Fl, Cl, Hn, 2 Vn, Va, Vc, Db, Hp (9)
Edicije Društva Slovenskih Skladateljev

Ramovš, Primož
1921

Enneaphonia
Fl, Cl, Bn, Vn, Va, Vc, Hp, P, Per (9)
DSS Editions

Rasmussen, Karl Aage
1947

Movements on a Moving Line
Fl, Ob, Cl, Bn, Hn, Trp, Trb, Per, P, 2 Vn, Va, Vc, Db (14)
Wilhelm Hansen Musik-Forlag

Rawsthorne, Alan
1905-71

Concerto for 10 Instruments
Fl, Ob/Eh, Cl, Bn, Hn, 2 Vn, Va, Vc, Db (10)
Oxford University Press

Read, Gardner
1913

Chorale and Fughetta, Op. 83A
4 Trp, 4 Hn, 3 Trb, 2 Eu, Tba (14)
Robert King Music Co.

Read, Gardner
1913

Sound Piece for Brass & Percussion, Op. 82
4 Trp, 4 Hn, 4 Trb, Eu, Tba (15)
Robert King Music Co.

Reck, David
1935

Number 1 for 12 Performers
Fl, Cl, Tsx, Hn, Va, Db, Gt, P, 4 Per (12)
MJQ Music, Inc.

Reed, Alfred
1921

Double Wind Quintet
Fl, Ob, Cl, Bn, 2 Hn, 2 Trp, Trb, Tba (10)
Edward B. Marks Music Corp.

Reiner, Karel
1910

Kleine Suite
Fl, 2 Ob, 2 Cl, 2 Bn, 2 Hn (9)
Český Hudební Fond

Reiter, Albert
1905-70

Musik für Bläser
3 Trp, 2 Hn, 2 Trb, Eu, Tba (9)
Ludwig Doblinger

Reizenstein, Franz
1911-68

Serenade
Fl, 2 Ob, 2 Cl, 2 Bn, 2 Trp, Db (10)
Musikverlag Hans Gerig

Revueltas, Silvestre
1899-1940

Homenaje a Federico García Lorca
Pic, Ecl, 2 Trp, Trb, Tba, Per, 2 Vn, Db, P (11)
McGinnis & Marx

Revueltas, Silvestre
1899-1940

Ocho por Radio
Cl, Bn, Trp, 2 Vn, Vc, Db, 3 Per (10)
Peer International

Revueltas, Silvestre
1899-1940

Planos, A Geometric Dance
Cl, Bcl, Bn, Trp, P, 2 Vn, Vc, Db (9)
Fleischer

Revueltas, Silvestre
1899-1940

Three Sonnets
2 Cl, 2 Trp, Hn, Per, Bcl, Bn, Tba, P (10)
Southern Music Pub. Co., Inc.

Reynolds, Roger
1934

Quick Are the Mouths of Earth
3 Fl/Pic, Ob, 3 Vc, Trp, 2 Trb, 2 Per, P (13)
C.F. Peters Corp.

Reynolds, Roger
1934

The Promises of Darkness
Fl, Cl, Bn, Hn, Trp, Trb, Vn, Vc, Db, P, Per (11)
C.F. Peters Corp.

Reynolds, Roger
1934

Wedge
2 Fl, 2 Trp, 2 Trb, Per, Db, P, (9)
C.F. Peters Corp.

Reynolds, Verne
1926

Prelude and Allegro
3 Trp, 4 Hn, 3 Trb, 2 Eu, Tba, Per (14)
Robert King Music Co.

Reynolds, Verne
1926

Theme and Variations
3 Trp, 3 Hn, 3 Trb, Eu, Tba, Per (12)
Robert King Music Co.

Rheinberger, Joseph
1839-1901

Nonet, Op. 139
Fl, Ob, Cl, Bn, Hn, Vn, Va, Vc, Db (9)
Musica Rara

Ricci-Signorini, Antonio
1867-1965

Fantasia Burlesca in C Major
Fl, Ob, Hn, Bn, 2 Per, P4h (9)
Carisch S.P.A.

Řídký, Jaroslav
1897-1956

Nonett, Op. 32
Fl, Ob, Cl, Bn, Hn, Vn, Va, Vc, Db (9)
Sadlova Edice

Riegger, Wallingford
1885-1961

Nonet
3 Trp, 2 Hn, 3 Trb, Tba (9)
Associated Music Publishers

Riegger, Wallingford
1885-1961

Study in Sonority, Op. 7
10 Vn (10)
Associated Music Publishers

Rieti, Vittorio
1898

Madrigal in Four Movements
Fl, Ob, Cl, Bn, Hn, Trp, 2 Vn, Va, Vc (10)
Andraud

Rochberg, George 1918

Chamber Symphony for 9 Instruments
Ob, Cl, Bn, Hn, Trp, Trb, Vn, Va, Vc (9)
Theodore Presser

Rochberg, George 1918

Music for the Magic Theater
Fl, Ob, Cl, Bn, 2 Hn, Trp, Trb, Tba, P, 2 Vn, Va, Vc, Db (15)
Theodore Presser

Rosetti, Francesco Antonio 1750-92

La Chasse
Fl, 2 Ob, 2 Hn, 2 Trp, Bn, 2 Vn, Va, Db (12)
Sieber

Rosetti, Francesco Antonio 1750-92

Partita in F
2 Fl, 2 Ob, 2 Cl, 2 Bn, 3 Hn, Db (12)
Cambridge Music Shop

Rosetti, Francesco Antonio 1750-92

Six Symphonies
Fl, 2 Ob, 2 Hn, 2 Vn, Va, Db (9)
Fétis

Rosetti, Francesco Antonio 1750-92

Three Symphonies, Op. 5
Fl, 2 Ob, 2 Hn, 2 Vn, Va, Db (9)
Fétis

Rosetti, Francesco Antonio 1750-92

Two Symphonies, Op. 13
Fl, 2 Ob, 2 Hn, 2 Vn, Va, Db (9)
Fétis

Rosseau, Norbert 1907-75

Fanfare, Op. 58
3 Trp, 4 Hn, 3 Trb, Tba, Per (12)
Centre Belge de Documentation Musicale

Rovics, Howard 1936

Events II
Ob, 2 Cl/Bcl, Trp, Vn, Vc, Db, P, 2 Per (10)
American Composers Alliance

Rovsing Olsen, Poul 1922

Patet per Nove Musici, Op. 55
Fl, Cl, Vn, Va, Vc, Gt, 3 Per (9)
Bote & Bock

Rowland, David 1939

Tropisms
Fl, Ob, Cl, Bn, Hn, Bcl, Trp, Trb, Per, P (10)
Stichting Donemus

Roy, Klaus 1924

Tripartita, Op. 5
3 Trp, 2 Hn, 3 Trb, 2 Eu, Tba (11)
Robert King Music Co.

Ruders, Poul 1949

4 Compositions
Fl/Afl, Cl/Bcl, Hn, P, 2 Vn, Va, Vc, Db (9)
Wilhelm Hansen Musik-Forlag

Ruders, Poul
1949

4 Dances in 1 Movement
Fl/Pic, Ob/Eh, Cl, Bn, Hn, Trp, Trb, Per, P, 2 Vn, Va, Vc, Db (14)
Wilhelm Hansen Musik-Forlag

Ruders, Poul
1949

Nightshade
Afl/Pic, Ob, Bcl, Cbn, Hn, Trb, Per, P, Vn, Db (10)
Wilhelm Hansen Musik-Forlag

Ruders, Poul
1949

Psalmodies
Gt, Ob, Cl, Bn, Hn, 2 Vn, Va, Vc, Db (10)
Wilhelm Hansen Musik-Forlag

Rudziński, Witold
1913

Nonet
Fl, Ob, Cl, Bn, Hn, Vn, Va, Vc, Db (9)
Polskie Wydawnictwo Muzyczne

Rudziński, Zbigniew
1935

Sonata
4 Vn, 2 Va, 2 Vc, P, Per (10)
Polskie Wydawnictwo Muzyczne

Ruyneman, Daniel
1886-1963

Hieroglyphs
3 Fl, Cel, P, 2 Gt, 2 Man, Per (10)
Stichting Donemus

Rychlik, Józef
1946

Africky Cyklus
Fl, Ob, Cl, Bn, 2 Hn, 2 Trb, P (9)
Editio Supraphon

Rychlik, Józef
1946

Symphonic Music I
4 Vn, 2 Va, 2 Vc, 2 P (10)
Polskie Wydawnictwo Muzyczne

Rydman, Kari
1836

Khoros No. 1
3 Fl, Ob, Vn, Va, Vc, Db, Hp, Per (10)
Musiikin Tiedotuskeskus

Saint-Saëns, Camille
1835-1921

Deuxième Suite
2 Fl, Ob, 2 Cl, 2 Bn, 2 Hn (9)
Baxter-Northrup

Saint-Saëns, Camille
1835-1921

Le Carnaval Des Animaux
Fl, Cl, 2 Vn, Va, Vc, Db, 2 P, 2 Per (11)
Durand & Cie

Salieri, Antonio
1750-1825

Two Wind Serenades
2 Fl, 2 Ob, 2 Hn, 2 Bn, Db (9)
S. Eugene Bailey

Salviucci, Giovanni
1907-37

Serenata
2 Vn, Va, Vc, Fl, Ob, Cl, Bn, Trp (9)
G. Ricordi & Co.

Salzedo, Leonard
1921

Diferencias, Op. 95
Hn, 4 Trp, 4 Trb, Tba (10)
Chester Music Limited

Samazeuilh, Gustave
1877-1967

Divertissement and Musette
Fl, Ob, Cl, Bn, Hn, 2 Vn, Va, Vc (9)
Durand & Cie

Samuel, Gerhard
1924

Cold When the Drum Sounds for Dawn
Fl/Pic/Afl, 2 Ob/Eh, 2 Hn, Bn, 2 Vn, Va, Vc, Db, Per, Hpd/Cel (13)
Belwin-Mills Company

Santoro, Claudio
1914

Intermitencias II
Fl, Ob, Cl, Bn, Hn, Trp, Trb, 2 Per, Vn, Va, Vc, Db (13)
Jobert & Cie

Satie, Erik
1866-1925

Messe Des Pauvres
Fl, Cl, Bcl, Bn, Hn, Trp, Trb, P, Hp, Vn, Vc, 2 Per (13)
Editions Salabert

Saxton, Robert
1953

Double Quintet
Fl, Ob, Cl, Bn, 2 Hn, 2 Trp, Trb, Tba (10)
Associated Music Publishers

Saxton, Robert
1953

Reflections of Narziss & Goldmund
Fl/Afl, Ob, Cl, Asx, Hn, Trp, Trb, 2 Va, Vc, Db, Hp, P/Cel (13)
J. & W. Chester Ltd.

Schäfer, Karl
1899-1970

Spielmusik
3 Cl, Vn, Vc, Db, 3 Per (9)
Heinrichshofen Verlag

Schäffer, Bogusław
1929

Permutationen
Fl, Ob, Cl, Asx, Trp, Trb, Va, Per, Hp, P (10)
Ahn & Simrock

Schibler, Armin
1920-86

Prologue
2 Fl, 2 Ob, 2 Cl, Bcl, 2 Bn, Cbn (10)
Ahn & Simrock

Schibler, Armin
1920-86

Signal, Beschwörung
2 Fl, 2 Ob, Eh, 2 Cl, Bcl, 2 Bn (10)
Ahn & Simrock

Schifrin, Lalo
1932

Ritual of Sound
Fl, Cl, Bcl, Hn, 2 Trp, Trb, Tba, Gt, 2 Db, 2 Per (13)
MJQ Music, Inc.

Schildknecht, Bjorn
1905-46

Fugerat Forspel
2 Fl, 2 Ob, 2 Cl, Bn, 2 Hn (9)
STIMS Informationscentral för Svensk Musik

Schiller, Henryk
1931

Music No. 2
Fl, 2 Cl, Bn, Trp, 4 Per, P, Vn, Vc, Db (13)
Sesac, Incorporated

Schiske, Karl
1916

Divertimento, Op. 49
Cl, Bn, Hn, Trp, Trb, 2 Vn, Va, Vc, Db (10)
Ludwig Doblinger

Schmitt, Franz
1874-1939

Fanfare, Le Camp de Pompée, Op. 69
3 Trp, 4 Hn, 3 Trb, Tba, 3 Per (14)
Uniunea Compozitorilor

Schmitt, Franz
1874-1939

Tullnerbacher Blasmusik
2 Ob, 3 Hn, 2 Trp, Tba, Per (9)
Ludwig Doblinger

Schoeck, Othmar
1886-1957

Serenade, Op. 1
Fl, Ob, Cl, Bn, Hn, 2 Vn, Va, Vc (9)
Hug & Company

Schoenberg, Arnold
1874-1951

Chamber Symphony, Op. 9
Fl, Ob, Eh, 2 Cl, Bcl, Bn, Cbn, 2 Hn, 2 Vn, Va, Vc (14)
Universal Editions

Scholz, Richard
1880

Second Divertimento for 9 Winds
Fl, 2 Ob, 2 Cl, 2 Bn, 2 Hn (9)
Manuscript

Schönherr, Max
1903-84

Dance
Fl, Ob, 2 Cl, Bn, 2 Trp, Per, 2 Vn, Vc, Db (12)
Universal Editions

Schreck, Gustav
1849-1918

Nonett, Op. 40
2 Fl, Ob, 2 Cl, 2 Bn, 2 Hn (9)
Breitkopf & Härtel

Schubert, Franz
1797-1828

Eine Kleine Trauermusik
2 Cl, 2 Bn, Cbn, 2 Hn, 2 Trb (9)
Ensemble Publications

Schudel, Thomas
1937

Set No. 2
Fl, Ob, Cl, Bn, 2 Hn, 2 Trp, Trb, Tba (10)
Canadian Music Centre

Schuller, Gunther
1925

Abstraction
Asx, Gt, Per, 2 Vn, Va, Vc, 2Db (9)
MJQ Music, Inc.

Schuller, Gunther
1925

Atonal Jazz Study
Fl, Ob, Tsx, Bsx, 2 Hn, Trp, Trb, Tba, P, Db, Per (12)
G. Schirmer

Schuller, Gunther
1925

Atonal Study in Jazz
Fl, Ob, Asx, Tsx, Bsx, 2 Hn, Trp, Trb, Tba, P, Db, Per (13)
Margun Music, Inc.

Schuller, Gunther
1925

Automation
Fl, Cl, Tsx, Hn, Trb, P, Hp, Db, 2 Per (10)
MJQ Music, Inc.

Schuller, Gunther
1925

Double Quintet
Fl, Ob, Cl, Bn, 2 Hn, 2 Trp, Trb, Tba (10)
Associated Music Publishers

Schuller, Gunther
1925

Music From Yesterday in Fact
Fl, Bcl, Asx, Hn, Vn, Vc, Db, Trp, P, Per (10)
Margun Music, Inc.

Schuller, Gunther
1925

Progression in Tempo
Fl, Cl, 2 Vn, Va, Vc, Db, Gt, 2 Per (11)
MJQ Music, Inc.

Schuller, Gunther
1925

Transformation
Fl, Cl, Tsx, Bn, Hn, Trb, Hp, P, Db, 2 Per (11)
G. Schirmer

Schuller, Gunther
1925

Twelve by Eleven
Fl, Cl, Tsx, Hn, Trb, P, Hp, Db, 2 Per (10)
MJQ Music, Inc.

Schuller, Gunther
1925

Variants on a Theme of John Lewis
Fl, Asx/Fl, Gt, P, 2 Vn, Va, Vc, 2 Db, 2 Per (12)
MJQ Music, Inc.

Schuller, Gunther
1925

Variants on a Theme of Thelonious Monk
Fl, Asx, Asx/Fl/Bcl, P, Gt, 2 Vn, Va, Vc, 2 Db, 2 Per (13)
G. Schirmer

Schuman, William
1910-92

Night Journey
Fl, Ob, Cl, Bn, Hn, P, 4 Vn, 2 Va, 2 Vc, Db (15)
Merion Music

Schumann, Georg
1866-1952

Suite für Blechbläser und Pauken
4 Trp, 4 Hn, 5 Trb, Per (14)
Sirius-Verlag

Schwantner, Joseph
1943

Diaphonia Intervallum
Asx, Fl, P, 2 Vn, Va, 2 Vc, Db (9)
C.F. Peters Corp.

Schwartz, Elliott
1936

Concert Piece for Ten Players
Fl/Pic, Ob, Cl/Bcl, Bn, Hn, Vn, Va, Vc, Db, Per (10)
Tetra

Schwertsik, Kurt
1935

Musik von Mutterland
Fl, Ob, Cl, Bcl, Hn, Trb, Vn, Va, Vc, Db (10)
Ludwig Doblinger

Schwertsik, Kurt
1935

Salotto Romano, Op. 5
Bcl, Bsx, Bn, Hn, Trb, Tba, Per, Db, Vc, Gt (10)
Edition Modern

Sciarino, Salvatore
1947

Da un Divertimento
Fl, Ob, Cl, Bn, Hn, 2 Vn, Va, Vc, Db (10)
G. Ricordi & Co.

Sear, Walter
1930

Antiphony
Fl, Ob, Cl, Bn, 2 Hn, 2 Trp, Trb, Tba (10)
Cor Publishing Co.

Searle, Humphrey
1915

Sinfonietta, Op. 49
Fl/Pic, Ob, Cl, Bn, Hn, Vn, Va, Vc, Db (9)
Faber Music Ltd.

Searle, Humphrey
1915

Variations and Finale, Op. 34
Fl/Pic, Ob, Cl, Bn, Hn, 2 Vn, Va, Vc, Db (10)
Schott & Company, Ltd.

Seiffert, Max
1948

Serenata
2 Fl, 2 Ob, 2 Hn, 2 Vn, Va, Db (10)
Breitkopf & Härtel

Sekles, Bernhard
1872-1934

Serenade, Op. 14
Fl, Ob, Cl, Bn, Hn, 2 Vn, Va, Vc, Db, Hp (11)
Rahter

Shahan, Paul
1923

Leipzig Towers
4 Trp, 4 Hn, 4 Trb, Eu, Tba, Per (15)
Robert King Music Co.

Shahan, Paul
1923

Spectrums
4 Trp, 4 Hn, 4 Trb, Eu, Tba, Per (15)
Robert King Music Co.

Sheriff, Noam
1935

Music
3 Fl, 3 Ob, 3 Cl, 3 Bn, Trb, P, Db (15)
Israeli Music Institute

Shulman, Alan
1915

Top Brass, 6 Minutes for 12
4 Trp, 4 Hn, 3 Trb, Tba (12)
Templeton Pub. Co., Inc.

Silverman, Stanley
1938

Planh
Fl, Cl, Vn, Va, Vc, 2 Per, Gt, Man (9)
Belwin-Mills Company

Siqueira, José de Lima
1907

Pregao for Eleven Instruments
Fl, Ob, Cl, Bn, Hn, P, 2 Vn, Va, Vc, Db (11)
Boletin Latinoamericano De Musica

Sixta, Jozef
1940

Noneto
Fl, Ob, Cl, Bn, Hn, 2 Vn, Va, Vc (9)
Slovensky Hudobny Fond

Skalkottas, Nikos
1904-49

Andante Sostenuto
Fl/Pic, Ob, Cl, Bn, Hn, Eh, Cbn, Trp, Trb, Tba, 2 Per (12)
Universal Editions

Škvor, František
1898-1970

Nonet II Prazsky
Fl, Ob, Cl, Bn, Hn, Vn, Va, Vc, Db (9)
Cesky Hudebni Fond

Škvor, František
1898-1970

Nonetto in B Minor
Fl, Ob, Cl, Bn, Hn, Vn, Va, Vc, Db (9)
Ceský Hudební Fond

Smalley, Roger
1943

Missa Parodia II
Fl/Pic, Ob, Cl, Hn, Trp, Trb, Vn, Va, P (9)
Faber Music Ltd.

Soegijo, Paul
1934

To Catch A Fly
Pic, Fl, Cl, Trp, Trb, Vn, Va, Vc, P, 3 Per (12)
Bote & Bock

Sollberger, Harvey
1938

Chamber Variations
2 Fl, Ob, Cl, Bsn, Vn, Va, Vc, Db, P, 2 Per (12)
American Composers Alliance

Sørensen, Bent
1958

Clairobscur
Fl, Ob/Eh, Cl, Bn, Hn, 2 Vn, Va, Vc, Db (10)
Wilhelm Hansen Musik-Forlag

Sørensen, Bent
1958

Shadowland
Fl, Ob, Cl, Bn, Hn, 2 Vn, Va, Vc, Db (10)
Wilhelm Hansen Musik-Forlag

Southers, Leroy, Jr.
1941

Concert Piece
Fl, Ob, Cl, Bn, Hn, 2 Vn, Va, Vc, Db, Hp, Per (12)
Canadian Music Centre

Spaeth, Sigmund
1885-1940

Divertimento
2 Hn, 2 Fl, 2 Ob, 2 Bn, 2 Vn, Db (11)
Breitkopf & Härtel

Spies, Claudio
1925

LXXXV
4 Cl, Bcl, 3 Vn, 3 Va, Vc (12)
Boosey & Hawkes

Spino, Pasquale
1942

Slow Waltz for Ten Brass
3 Trp, 3 Trb, 3 Hn, Tba (10)
Standard Music Publishers

Spohr, Ludwig
1784-1859

Nonet in F, Op. 31
Fl, Ob, Cl, Bn, Hn, Vn, Va, Vc, Db (9)
H. Litolff's Verlag

Sporck, Georges
1870-1943

Landscapes of Normandy
2 Fl, 2 Ob, 2 Cl, 2 Bn, 2 Hn (10)
Andraud

Šrom, Karel
1904-81

Märchen
Fl, Ob, Cl, Bn, Hn, Vn, Va, Vc, Db (9)
Editio Supraphon

Stabile, James
1937

Suite
6 Trp, 6 Trb, Tba, Per (14)
Western International Music

Stachowiak, Lechosław
1926

Three Improvisations
3 Fl, 3 Cl, 2 Hn, 2 Vn, Va, Vc (12)
Ars Polona

Stamitz, Karl
1746-1801

La Chasse
Fl, 2 Ob, 2 Bn, 2 Hn, 2 Trp, 2 Vn, Va, Db (13)
Sieber

Stanford, Charles
1852-1924

Serenade for String & Winds, Op. 95
Fl, Cl, 2 Bn, Hn, Vn, Va, Vc, Db (9)
Andraud

Starer, Robert
1924

Serenade for Brass
3 Trp, 4 Hn, 3 Trb, Tba (11)
Southern Music Pub. Co., Inc.

Stearns, Peter
1931

Serenade
3 Fl, 3 Ob, 3 Cl, 2 Bn, 3 Hn, Tba (15)
American Composers Alliance

Steffen, Wolfgang
1923

Festliche Fanfare
4 Trp, 4 Trb, Tba, (9)
Sirius-Verlag

Steiner, Gitta
1932

Movements
Fl, 2 Cl, Hn, Trp, Trb, Tba, Vn, Va, Vc (10)
Seesaw Music Corp.

Stewart, Robert
1825-94

Music for Brass No. 4
4 Trp, 2 Hn, 3 Trb, Eu, Tba (11)
American Composers Alliance

Stewart, Robert
1825-94

Nonet
Fl, Cl, Bn, Hn, Trp, Vn, Va, Vc, P (9)
American Composers Alliance

Stewart, Robert
1825-94

Two Ricercari
Fl, Ob, Cl, Bn, Hn, 2 Vn, Va, Vc (9)
Composers Facsimile Edition

Stockhausen, Karlheinz
1928

Kontra-Punkte No. 1
Fl, Cl, Bcl, Bn, Trp, Trb, P, Hp, Vn, Vc (10)
Universal Editions

Stöhr, Richard
1874-1967

Kammersymphonie, Op. 32
2 Vn, Va, Vc, Ob, Cl, Hn, Bn, Hp (9)
Kahnt

Stolte, Siegfried
1925

Fanfare des Friedens
3 Trp, 2 Hn, 3 Trb, Tba, Per (10)
Musica Rara

Stout, Alan
1932

Pieta
6 Trp, 3 Trb, Tba (10)
European American Music

Strandberg, Newton
1921

Verses for Five
Pic, Fl, Afl, Cl, Bcl, Vn, Va, Vc, P (9)
Manuscript Publications

Strauss, Richard
1864-1949

Orchesterstudien für Wind Inst.
3 Cl, Ob, 2 Eh, Hn, Tba, Trp, Btrp, Bn, Cbn (12)
C.F. Peters Corp.

Strauss, Richard
1864-1949

Serenade for Woodwinds
2 Fl, 2 Cl, 2 Bn, 4 Hn (10)
International Music Company

Strauss, Richard
1864-1949

Serenade, Op. 7
2 Fl, 2 Ob, 2 Cl, 2 Bn, 4 Hn, Cb(Tba) (13)
International Music Company

Strauss, Richard
1864-1949

Suite
2 Fl, 2 Ob, 2 Cl, 2 Bn, 4 Hn (12)
McGinnis & Marx

Strauss, Richard
1864-1949

Suite, Op. 4
2 Fl, 2 Ob, 2 Cl, 2 Bn, Cbn, 4 Hn (13)
F.E.C. Leuckart Verlag

Stravinsky, Igor
1882-1972

Concertino for 12 Instruments
Fl, Ob, Eh, Cl, 2 Bn, 2 Trp, 2 Trb, Vn, Vc (12)
Wilhelm Hansen Musik-Forlag

Stravinsky, Igor
1882-1972

Dumbarton Oaks Concerto
Fl, Cl, Bn, 2 Hn, 3 Vn, 3 Va, 2 Vc, 2 Db (15)
Cambridge Music Shop

Stravinsky, Igor
1882-1972

Eight Instrumental Miniatures
2 Fl, 2 Ob, 2 Cl, 2 Bn, Hn, 2 Vn, 2 Va, 2 Vc (15)
Chester Music Limited

Stravinsky, Igor
1882-1972

Ragtime
Fl, Cl, Hn, Trp, Trb, 2 Vn, Va, Db, 2 Per (11)
J. & W. Chester Ltd.

Stravinsky, Igor
1882-1972

Song of Hauleurs on the Volga
Pic, Fl, Ob, Cl, Bn, 2 Hn, 3 Trp, Tba, Per (12)
J. & W. Chester Ltd.

Striegler, Kurt
1886-1958

Kammer-Sinfonie, Op. 14
Fl, Ob, Cl, Bn, Hn, 2 Vn, Va, Vc, Db (10)
Junne

Striegler, Kurt
1886-1958

Nonet, Op. 14
Fl, Ob, Cl, Bn, Hn, 2 Vn, Va, Vc (9)
Junne

Stringham, Edwin
1990-74

Nocturne
2 Fl, 2 Ob, 2 Cl, 2 Bn, 2 Hn, Hp, Acl (12)
Fleischer

Štuhec, Igor
1932

Ction
Fl, Cl, Hn, Trp, Trb, Vn, Vc, Db, P, Hp, Per (11)
Edicije Društva Slovenskih Skladateljev

Stürmer, Bruno
1892-1958

Suite
3 Vn, Vc, Db, Fl, Cl, P4h, Hrm (10)
C.F. Vieweg Musikverlag

Stürmer, Bruno
1892-1958

Suite in G Minor, Op. 9
Fl, Ob, Cl, Bn, 2 Vn, Va, Vc, Db (9)
Schott

Sumerlin, Macon
1919

Fanfare, Andante & Fugue
2 Trp, 3 Hn, 3 Trb, Tba, Per (10)
Western International Music

Surinach, Carlos
1915

Hieroglyphics
2 Fl, 2 Pic, Eh, 2 Cl, Bcl, Hn, 4 Vc, 2 Db (15)
Associated Music Publishers

Sutermeister, Heinrich
1910

Modeste Mignon Nach Einem Walzer
2 Fl, 2 Ob, Ecl, Cl, 2 Hn, 2 Bn (10)
B. Schotts' Söhne

Szabelski, Boleslaw
1896-1979

Aphorisms 9
Fl, Ob, Cl, Trp, Trb, Per, Vn, Va, Vc (9)
Polskie Wydawnictwo Muzyczne

Szymanski, Pawel
1954

Quasi una Sinfonietta
Fl/Pic, Ob, Cl, Bn, Hn, Trp, Trb, Per, P, 2 Vn, Va, Vc, Db (14)
Chester Music Limited

Takahashi, Yuji
1938

Bridges II
2 Ob, 2 Cl, 2 Trp, 3 Va (9)
C.F. Peters Corp.

Takemitsu, Toru
1930

The Dorian Horizon, Echores
6 Vn, 3 Db (9)
Ongaku Notomo Sha Corp.

Tanenbaum, Elias
1924

29526 T
Pic/Fl/Afl, Cl/Asx, Bn, Trp, Trb, Vn, Db, P, Per (9)
American Composers Alliance

Tanenbaum, Elias
1924

Trios I, II, III
Asx, Hn, Trp, Trb, Vn, Va, Vc, Db, Per (9)
American Composers Alliance

Taneyev, Alexander
1850-1918

Andante for Double Woodwind Quintet
2 Fl, 2 Ob, 2 Cl, 2 Bn, 2 Hn (10)
McGinnis & Marx

Taraba, Bohuslav
1894

Three Meditations
Fl, Ob, Cl, 2 Bn, Hn, 2 Vn, Va, Vc (10)
Ceský Hudebni Fond

Tarenskeen, Boudewijn
1952

Machtelt Suite
2 Asx, 2 Tsx, Hn, 2 trp, 3 trb, Db (11)
Stichting Donemus

Taub, Bruce
1948

Chamber Variations 4
Fl, Ob, Cl, Bn, Trb, Vn, Va, Vc, Db, P, Per (11)
American Composers Alliance

Tavener, John
1944

Grandma's Footsteps
Ob, Bn, Hn, 6 Vn, 2 Va, 2 Vc (13)
J. & W. Chester Ltd.

Taylor, Clifford
1923-87

Five Poems
Ob, Hn, Trp, Trb, Tba, 2 Vn, 2 Va, Vc (10)
American Composers Alliance

Taylor, Clifford
1923-87

Inscriptions in Brass
3 Trp, 4 Hn, 3 Trb, Eu, Tba, Per (13)
G. Schirmer

Tcherepnin, Ivan
1943

Wheelwinds
2 Fl, Afl, Ob, Eh, Ecl, Cl, Bcl, Bn (9)
B. Schotts' Söhne

Tcherepnin, Nikolai
1873-1945

Fanfare
3 Trp, 4 Hn, 3 Trb, Tba, Per (12)
Boosey & Hawkes

Tcherepnin, Nikolai
1873-1945

Sonatine, Op. 61
2 Fl, 2 Ob, Cl, 2 Bn, Hn, 2 Trp, Trb, 2 Per (13)
M.P. Belaieff

Thärichen, Werner
1921

Bläsermusik, Op. 43
4 Trp, 4 Trb, Tba (9)
Bote & Bock

Thomsen, Geraldine
1917

Nonett
Fl, Ob, Cl, Bn, Hn, Vn, Va, Vc, Db (9)
Ceský Hudební Fond

Tippett, Michael
1905

Fanfare No. 1
3 Trp, 4 Hn, 3 Trb (10)
B. Schotts' Söhne

Tippett, Michael
1905

Praeludium
3 Trp, 6 Hn, 3 Trb, 2 Tba, Per (15)
B. Schotts' Söhne

Tisne, Antoine
1932

Caractères
Fl, Ob, Cl, Bn, Hn, 2 Vn, Va, Vc, Db, Per (11)
Billaudot Editions Musicales

Töeschi, Carl Joseph
1731-88

Partita Notturna
2 Cl, 2 Hn, 2 Va, 2 Vc, Db (9)
Mannheimer Musik-Verlag

Töeschi, Johann
1735-1800

Three Symphonies, Op. 7
2 Ob, 2 Bn, 2 Hn, 2 Vn, Va, Db (10)
Fétis

Tomasi, Henri-Frédien
1901-71

Fanfares Liturgiques
3 Trp, 4 Hn, 4 Trb, Tba, Per (13)
Alphonse Leduc

Tomasi, Henri-Frédien
1901-71

Jeux de Geishas
Fl, Ob, Cl, Bn, Hn, 2 Vn, Va, Vc, Hp, Per (11)
Durand & Cie

Tower, Joan
1938

Third Fanfare for the Uncommon Woman
4 Trp, 2 Hn, 2 Trb, 2 Tba (10)
Associated Music Publishers

Tremblay, George
1911-82

Champs II (Souffles)
2 Fl, Ob, Cl, Hn, 2 Trp, 2 Trb, Db, P, Per (12)
Canadian Music Centre

Tremblay, George
1911-82

Champs III (Vers)
2 Fl, Cl, Trp, Hn, 3 Vn, Db, 3 Per (12)
Canadian Music Centre

Tremblay, George
1911-82

Sérénade
Fl, Cl, Bn, Hn, Trp, 2 Vn, Va, Vc, Db, P, Per (12)
American Composers Alliance

Trimble, Lester
1920-86

Concerto
Fl, Ob, Cl, Bn, 2 Vn, Va, Vc, Db (9)
C.F. Peters Corp.

Trimble, Lester
1920-86

Panels I
Pic, Bsx, Vn, Va, Vc, Db, 2 Per, Egt, Eorg, Ehpd (11)
C.F. Peters Corp.

Trombly, Preston
1945

Chamber Concerto
Fl, Ob, Cl, Hn, Trp, Trb, Vn, Va, Db, P, Hp, Per (12)
American Composers Alliance

Turner, Robert
1920

Variations and Toccata
Fl, Ob, Cl, Bn, Hn, 2 Vn, Va, Vc, Db (10)
Canadian Music Centre

Turok, Paul
1929

Elegy in Memory of K. Rathaus
3 Trp, 2 Hn, 3 Trb, Eu, Tba (12)
Musica Rara

Über, Christian Benjamin
1746-1812

Serenata
2 Fl, 2 Ob, 2 Cl, 2 Bn, 2 Hn, 2 Vn, 2 Va, Db (15)
Breitkopf & Härtel

Über, Christian Benjamin
1746-1812

Serenata
3 Vn, 2 Hn, 2 Fl, Va, Db (9)
Breitkopf & Härtel

Uber, David
1921

Canzona Moderna in Homage to G. Gabrieli
4 Trp, 2 Hn, 3 Trb, Eu, 2 Tba (12)
Standard Music Publishers

Uber, David
1921

Evolution I
4 Trp, 4 Hn, 3 Trb, Eu, Tba, Per (14)
Southern Music Pub. Co., Inc.

Uber, David
1921

Gloria in Excelsis
4 Trp, 2 Hn, 3 Trb, Eu, Tba, Per (12)
Standard Music Publishers

Uber, David
1921

Liturgy, Op. 50
4 Trp, 2 Hn, 3 Trb, Eu, Tba, Per (12)
Ensemble Publications

Uber, David
1921

The Power and the Glory, Prelude
4 Trp, 2 Hn, 3 Trb, Eu, Tba, Per (12)
Southern Music Pub. Co., Inc.

Uber, David
1921

The Power and the Glory, Ritual Dance
4 Trp, 2 Hn, 3 Trb, Eu, Tba, Per (12)
Southern Music Pub. Co., Inc.

Uber, David
1921

The Power and the Glory, Spiritual
4 Trp, 2 Hn, 3 Trb, Eu, Tba, Per (12)
Southern Music Pub. Co., Inc.

Uber, David
1921

Twentieth Century Antiphonal, Op. 38
4 Trp, 4 Hn, 3 Trb, Eu, 2 Tba (14)
Southern Music Pub. Co., Inc.

Urbanner, Erich
1936

Improvisation III
Fl, Ob, Cl, Bn, 2 Vn, Va, Vc, Db, Per (10)
Ludwig Doblinger

Urbanner, Erich
1936

Lyrica
Fl, Cl, Hn, Trb, Vn, Db, Hp, Cel, P, Per (10)
Ludwig Doblinger

Valcárcel, Teodoro
1900-42

Dicotomia III
2 Trp, 2 Hn, 2 Trb, 2 Vn, 2 Va, 2 Vc (12)
Southern Music Pub. Co., Inc.

Van der Velden, Renier
1910

Etude
Fl, Ob, Cl, Bn, Hn, Trp, Trb, Va, Vc, Db, P (11)
CeBeDem

Van der Velden, Renier
1910

Fanfare
3 Trp, 4 Hn, 3 Trb, Tba, Per (12)
Centre Belge de Documentation Musicale

Van der Velden, Renier
1910

Les Ancêtres
Fl, Ob, Cl, Bn, 2 Hn, 2 Vc, Db (10)
CeBeDem

Varèse, Edgard
1883-1965

Hyperprism
Fl, Cl, 3 Hn, 2 Trp, 2 Trb, Per (10)
E.C. Kerby, Ltd.

Varèse, Edgard
1883-1965

Intégrales
2 Fl, Ob, 2 Cl, Hn, 2 Trp, Trb, 2 Tba, Per (12)
E.C. Kerby, Ltd.

Vaughan Williams, Ralph
1872-1959

Scherzo alla Marcia
Fl, Pic, 2 Ob, 2 Cl, 2 Bn, 2 Hn, 2 Trp, 3 Trb (15)
Oxford University Press

Veress, Sándor
1907

Musica Concertante
7 Vn, 2 Va, 2 Vc, Db (12)
Edizioni Suvini Zerboni

Vernon, W. Knight
1934

Suite
3 Trp, 3 Hn, 3 Trb, Per (10)
G. Schirmer

Verrall, John
1908

Nonette
Fl, Ob, Cl, Bn, Hn, 2 Vn, Va, Vc (9)
Composers Facsimile Edition

Vlad, Roman
1919

Serenata
Fl, 2 Ob, 2 Cl, 2 Bn, 2 Hn, 2 Va, Cel (12)
Edizioni Suvini Zerboni

Vogt, Hans
1911

Concertino
Trp, 2 Hn, Fl, Ob, 2 Cl, 2 Bn, Per, P (11)
Bärenreiter Verlag

Volans, Kevin
1949

Chevron
2 Fl, Ob, Cl, Bcl, Bn, Hn, Trp, Trb, P, 2 Vn, Va, Vc (14)
Chester Music Limited

Vomáčka, Boleslav
1887-1965

Nonett
Fl, 2 Ob, 2 Cl, 2 Bn, 2 Hn (9)
Český Hudební Fond

Vostřák, Zbynek
1920-85

Tao
Fl, Ob, Cl, Bn, 2 Per, Vn, Va, Vc, Db (10)
Universal Editions

Vranicky, Pavel
1756-1808

Jägermärsche
2 Fl, 2 Ob, 2 Cl, 2 Bn, 2 Hn, Cbn, Trp (10)
Artia

Vriend, Jan
1938

Paroesie
Fl, Bn, Hn, Trp, Vn, Db, Hp, P, 2 Per (10)
Stichting Donemus

Vries, Klaas de
1944

Moeilijkheden
Fl, 2 Asx, Hn, 2 Trp, 3 Trb, P (10)
Stichting Donemus

Wagner, Richard
1813-83

Siegfried Idyll
Fl, Ob, 2 Cl, Bn, 2 Hn, Trp, 2 Vn, Va, Vc, Db (13)
Edwin F. Kalmus

Walton, William 1902-83	**Fanfare for the Queen** 8 Trp, 4 Trb (12) Oxford University Press
Wanek, Friedrich K. 1929	**Vier Grotesken** 2 Fl, 2 Ob, 2 Cl, 2 Bn, 2 Hn, Trp, Per (12) Schott
Wanhal, Johann Baptiste 1739-1813	**Sinfonia in G Minor** 2 Ob, 4 Hn, 2 Vn, Va, Vc, Db (11) Ludwig Doblinger
Ward, William 1918	**Fantasia** 3 Trp, 4 Hn, 3 Trb, Tba, Per (12) Highgate Press
Warren, Raymond 1928	**Music for Harlequin** 2 Trp, 2 Hn, 2 Trb, Fl, Ob, 2 Cl, Per (11) Musica Rara
Washburn, Robert 1928	**Concertino** Fl, Ob, Cl, Bn, 2 Hn, 2 Trp, Trb, Tba (10) Oxford University Press
Weber, Carl Maria von 1786-1826	**March for Harmonie** 2 Trp, 2 Hn, Trb, Fl, 2 Ob, 2 Cl, 2 Bn (12) Musica Rara
Weber, Carl Maria von 1786-1826	**Marcia Vivace** 10 Trp, Per (11) Albert J. Kunzelmann
Webern, Anton von 1883-1945	**Concerto, Op. 24** Fl, Ob, Cl, Hn, Trp, Trb, Vn, Va, P (9) Universal Editions
Webern, Anton von 1883-1945	**Sinfonie, Op. 21** Cl, Bcl, 2 Hn, Hp, 2 Vn, Va, Vc (9) Universal Editions
Welin, Karl-Erik 1934	**NR 3** Fl, Ob, Cl, Bcl, Hn, Trp, Trb, Vn, Db (9) N. Simrock
Werdin, Ebern 1911	**Konzertante Musik** 2 Vn, Va, Db, 4 Rec (9) Heinrichshofen Verlag
Werle, Lars Johan 1926	**Summer Music** 6 Vn, 2 Va, 2 Vc, Db, P (12) J. & W. Chester Ltd.

Whittenberg, Charles
1927-84

Variations for Nine
Fl, Ob, Cl, Bn, Hn, Trp, Trb, Vn, Db (9)
C.F. Peters Corp.

Wijdeveld, Wolfgang
1910-85

Concertpiece
Fl, Ob, Cl, Bn, Hn, 3 Vn, 2 Va, 2 Vc, Db (13)
Stichting Donemus

Wilder, Alec
1907-80

A Debutante's Diary
Fl, Ob, 2 Cl, Bcl, Eh(Asx), Bn, P, Db, Per (10)
Kendor Music, Inc.

Williams, Evans
1920

Fant'sy II
Fl, 2 Ob, Cl, Bn, Trp, Trb, 2 Vn, Va, Vc, Per (12)
Boelke-Bomart Publications

Wilson, George
1927

Concatenations
Fl, Cl, Bcl, Hn, Trp, Trb, Vn, Vc, Db, Per, Acc, Egt (12)
Jobert & Cie

Wiszniewski, Zbigniew
1922

Chamber Music No. 4
Fl, Ob, Cl, Bn, Hn, Vn, Va, Vc, Db, P (10)
Polskie Wydawnictwo Muzyczne

Wolf-Ferrari, Ermanno
1876-1948

Kammersymphonie, Op. 8
Fl, Ob, Cl, Bn, Hn, 2 Vn, Va, Vc, P (10)
Andraud

Wolff, Christian
1934

Nine
Fl, Cl, Hn, Trp, Trb, 2 Vc, Cel, P (9)
C.F. Peters Corp.

Wolpe, Stefan
1902-72

Chamber Piece No. 1
Ob, 3 Fl, 3 Vc, Trp, 2 Trb, P, 2 Per (13)
C.F. Peters Corp.

Woollen, Russell
1923

Triptych, Op. 34
4 Trp, 2 Hn, 3 Trb, Tba (10)
C.F. Peters Corp.

Wuorinen, Charles
1938

Canzona
Fl, Ob/Eh, Cl/Bcl, Bn, Trp, Vn, Va, Vc, Db, Hp, Per, P (12)
C.F. Peters Corp.

Wuorinen, Charles
1938

Chamber Concerto
Fl, Db, P, Hp, Gt, Hpd, 5 Per (11)
C.F. Peters Corp.

Wuorinen, Charles
1938

The Winds
Fl, Ob, Cl, Bcl, Vn, Trp, Trb, Tba, P (9)
C.F. Peters Corp.

Wyttenbach, Jürg 1935	Divisions 4 Vn, 2 Va, 2 Vc, Db, P (10) Schott & Company, Ltd.
Xenakis, Iannis 1922	Analogique A 3 Vn, 3 Vc, 3 Db (9) E.F. M. Technisonor
Xenakis, Iannis 1922	Atrées Fl, Cl, Bcl, Hn, Trp, Trb, Per, Vn, Vc (9) Editions Salabert
Xenakis, Iannis 1922	Linaia-Agon. 3 Hn, 3 Trb, 3 Tba (9) Editions Salabert
Xenakis, Iannis 1922	Phlegra Fl/Pic, Ob, Cl/Bcl, Bn, Hn, Trp, Trb, Vn, Va, Vc, Db (11) Editions Salabert
Xenakis, Iannis 1922	ST/10-1,080262 Cl, Bcl, 2 Hn, 2 Vn, Va, Vc, Hp, Per (10) Boosey & Hawkes
Young, Lynden de 1923	Divertissement 4 Trp, 4 Hn, 3 Trb, Eu, Tba, Per (14) Robert King Music Co.
Yttrehus, Rolv 1926	Music for Winds, Percussion & Viola Fl/Pic, Bcl, Hn, Trp, Trb, Va, P, 2 Per (9) American Composers Alliance
Zádor, Eugen 1894-1977	Suite 4 Trp, 4 Hn, 3 Trb, Tba (12) Edition Eulenburg
Zaninelli, Luigi 1932	Jubilate Deo 4 Hn, 4 Trpt, 4 Trb, Tba (13) Shawnee Press, Inc
Zaninelli, Luigi 1932	Music for a Solemn Occasion 5 Trp, 4 Trb, Tba, Per (11) Theodore Presser
Zillig, Winfried 1905	Serenade No. 2 3 Cl, Hn, Trp, Trb, 2 Vn, Vc (9) Bärenreiter Verlag
Zillig, Winfried 1905	Serenade No. 4 Fl, Ob, Cl, Bn, Hn, Trp, Trb, Per, Cel, Cem, 2 Vn, Va, Vc, Db (15) Bärenreiter Verlag

Zimmermann, Gustav
1887-1926

Rheinische Kirmestänze
2 Fl, 2 Ob, 2 Cl, 2 Bn, 2 Hn, Trp, Trb, Tba (13)
B. Schotts' Söhne

Zindars, Earl
1927

The Brass Square
4 Trp, 4 Hn, 3 Trb, Tba, Per (13)
Robert King Music Co.

Zonn, Paul
1938

Canzonni, Overo Sonate Concertare Con-Serere
Fl, Ob, Trp, Fn, Trb, Db, P, Hp, Per (9)
American Composers Alliance

Zonn, Paul
1938

Sonorum I
Fl, Ob, Cl, Hn, Trp, Trb, Vn, Va, Db, 2 Per (11)
American Composers Alliance

THE REPERTORY CLASSIFIED

Compositions Including
String Combinations

Violin, Viola, Cello, and Double Bass

Albright, William .... Marginal Worlds
Alsina, Carlos ....Auftrag
Babbitt, Milton ....Composition for 12 Instruments
Babusek, František .... Noneto
Baervoets, Raymond .... Musica per 14 Strumenti
Benhamou, Maurice...Mizmor-Chir
Bentzon, Niels Viggo......................... Sonata for Twelve Instruments, Op. 257
Bořkovec, Pavel..Nonetto
Boykan, Martin .... Concerto
Bozay, Attila ....Serie, Op. 19
Bozay, Attila ....Sorozat
Bresgen, Cesar.. Kammerkonzert, Op. 6
Cordero, Roque...Paz-Paiz-Peace
Corghi, Azio ....Divertimento
Crosse, Gordon .... Ariadne
Custer, Arthur...Cycle for Nine Instruments
David, Thomas...Concerto for 9 Instruments
Davidovsky, Mario... Inflexions
Dobiáš, Václav ....O Rodne Zemi
Druckman, Jacob...Incenters
Eckhardt, Sophie-Carmen...Nonet
Edwards, George .... Bits
Erickson, Robert..Chamber Concerto
Farrenc, Jeanne Louise.. Nonetto, Op. 38

Feld, Jindřich ....Kammersuite
Feld, Jindřich ....Nonetto, Suite de Chambre
Flosman, Oldřich..Nonet No. 2
Foerster, Josef...Nonet
Folprecht, Zdeněk ....Concertino, Op. 21
Fritsch, Johannes .... Modulation II
Geissler, Fritz...Nonett
Gibson, Jon Charles .... Melody IV
Giefer, Willy ....Pro-Kontra
Giuranna, Bruno...Adagio e Allegro Da Concerto
Guinjoàn, Juan ....Improvisation I
Hába, Alois ....Nonet No. 1, Op. 40
Hába, Alois ....Nonet No. 3, Op. 82
Harbison, John ....Confinement
Heussenstam, George .... Seventeen Impressions from the Japanese, Op. 35
Hibbard, William ....Stabiles
Hindemith, Paul....................................... Concert Music, Op. 36, No. 1
Hlobil, Emil...Nonet, Op. 27
Hoch, Francesco..L'Oggetto Disincantato
Hoch, Francesco................................... Transparenza per Nuovi Elementi
Holmboe, Vagn .... Chamber Concerto No. 2, Op. 20
Ives, Charles.. Chromatimelotune
Janáček, Leoš...Mala Suite
Jaroch, Jiří... Detska Suita
Jaroch, Jiří... Kindersuite
Jaroch, Jiří... Nonetto II
Kahowez, Günter ....Bardo-Puls
Kalabis, Viktor.. Klasicky Nonet
Kirchner, Leon.. Music for Twelve
Klebanov, Demitri..Ukrainian Concertino
Klusák, Jan...Invention
Kopelent, Marek................................... Pocta Vladimiru Holanovi
Kox, Hans.. Cyclofony VIII
Kubik, Gail..Divertimento No. 1
Kubin, Rudolf...Nonetto
Kubizek, Augustin...................................... Quartetto da Camera, Op. 24a
Kubizek, Augustin...................................... Sinfonia da Camera, Op. 26b
Kučera, Václav.. Dramata
Kupferman, Meyer..Infinites 14
Lehmann, Hans...Quanti
Leibowitz, René ....Chamber Concerto, Op. 10
Leibowitz, René ....Chamber Symphony, Op. 16
Leibowitz, René ....Suite, Op. 81
Lieberson, Peter ....Lalita - Chamber Variations
Loeb, David...Partita da Camera
Lutoslawski, Witold.. Slides
Maes, Jef ....De Verloofden
Martinů, Bohuslav ....Nonetto
Marttinen, Tauno..Nonet
Maštalíř, Jaroslav...Nonetto

Matsushita, Shin-Ichi..Correlations for 3 Groups
Mikoda, Bořivoj... Nonetto, Op. 30
Milhaud, Darius... Aspen Serenade
Milhaud, Darius.. Musique pour Graz
Morthenson, Jan W...Antiphonia III
Nono, Luigi...Canti per 13
Novák, Jan .... Baletti a 9
Odstrčil, Karel .... Siluety
Olah, Tiberiu...Perspectives
Onslow, George.. Nonetto, Op. 77
Osterc, Slavko ....Nonet
Pauer, Ernst...Divertimento
Petrescu, Dinu.. Musique
Petrić, Ivo.. Inlaid-Work
Petrić, Ivo... Petit Concerto De Chambre
Phillips, Peter.. Chimer
Pierné, Gabriel..March of the Little Lead Soldiers
Poulenc, Francis...Mouvements Perpétuels
Powell, Mel... Modules
Rheinberger, Joseph... Nonet, Op. 139
Řídký, Jaroslav ....Nonett, Op. 32
Rudziński, Witold ....Nonet
Rydman, Kari... Khoros No. 1
Santoro, Claudio ....Intermitencias II
Schwartz, Elliott....................................Concert Piece for Ten Players
Schwertsik, Kurt .... Musik von Mutterland
Searle, Humphrey.. Sinfonietta, Op. 49
Škvor, František ....Nonet II Prazsky
Škvor, František .... Nonetto in B Minor
Sollberger, Harvey.. Chamber Variations
Šrom, Karel..Märchen
Stanford, Charles.............................. Serenade for String & Winds, Op. 95
Tanenbaum, Elias...Trios I, II, III
Taub, Bruce ....Chamber Variations 4
Thomsen, Geraldine..Nonett
Trimble, Lester..Panels I
Vostřák, Zbynek...Tao
Wiszniewski, Zbigniew............................... Chamber Music No. 4
Wuorinen, Charles..Canzona
Xenakis, Iannis.. Phlegra

2 Violin, Viola, Cello

Adaskin, Murray...................................Rondino for Nine Instruments
Antunes, Jorge...Intervertige
Bedford, David..Trona for 12
Bentzon, Niels Viggo.............................Climate Changes, Op. 474
Birtwistle, Harrison .... Tragoedia

Bland, William	Sonics I, II, III
Bogusławski, Edward	Intonazioni I
Brown, Jonathan Bruce	Fragments
Busch, Adolf	Divertimento
Casanova, André	Serenata
Castro, Christobal de	10 + 1
Caturla, Alejandro	Bembe
Fellagara, Vittorio	Serenata
Fleming, Robert	Maritime Suite
Gabichvadze, Revaz	Quick Motion
Geissler, Fritz	Ode an eine Nachtigall
Górecki, Henryk Mikolaj	Concerto, Op. 11
Guinjoàn, Juan	Fragment
Harsányi, Tibor	Nonett
Hauer, Josef	Dance Suite No. 1, Op. 70
Hauer, Josef	Dance Suite No. 2, Op. 71
Hauer, Josef	Zwölftonspiel
Hauer, Josef	Zwölftonspiel
Hess, Willy	Serenade, Op. 19
Homs, Joaquin	Musica Para 11
Ibert, Jacques	Capriccio
Lebič, Lojze	Kons (b)
Lewis, Peter	Lamentation, 3 Epigrams
Maksymiuk, Jerzy	Decet
Milhaud, Darius	Printemps
Mills, Charles	Chamber Concerto
Miroglio, Francis	Réseaux
Mozart, Wolfgang Amadeus	Galimathias Musicum, K. 32
Ordoñez, Carlos d'.	Five Chamber Symphonies
Pablo, Luis de	Modulos I
Pálsson, Páll	Crystals
Pittaluga, Gustavo	Petite Suite
Rieti, Vittorio	Madrigal in Four Movements
Salviucci, Giovanni	Serenata
Samazeuilh, Gustave	Divertissement and Musette
Schoeck, Othmar	Serenade, Op. 1
Schoenberg, Arnold	Chamber Symphony, Op. 9
Sixta, Jozef	Noneto
Stachowiak, Lechosław	Three Improvisations
Stewart, Robert	Two Ricercari
Stöhr, Richard	Kammersymphonie, Op. 32
Striegler, Kurt	Nonet, Op. 14
Taraba, Bohuslav	Three Meditations
Tomasi, Henri-Frédien	Jeux de Geishas
Verrall, John	Nonette
Volans, Kevin	Chevron
Webern, Anton von	Sinfonie, Op. 21
Wolf-Ferrari, Ermanno	Kammersymphonie, Op. 8
Xenakis, Iannis	ST/10-1,080262

2 Violins, Viola, Cello, and Double Bass

Abrahamsen, Hans..Geduldspiel
Abrahamsen, Hans...Lied in Fall
Abrahamsen, Hans..Märchenbilder
Adaskin, Murray...Rondino for Nine Instruments
Adler, Samuel...Concert Piece
Adler, Samuel...Divertimento
Adler, Samuel..Histrionics
Adler, Samuel...Music for Eleven
Adler, Samuel...Praeludium
Aitken, Hugh ....Serenade
Alpaerts, Flor...Treurdicht
Alsina, Carlos ....Auftrag
Alsina, Carlos ....Funktionen, Op. 14
Alwyn, William...Fanfare for a Joyful Occasion
Amato, Bruno ....Basses and Brass
Ameller, André-Charles.................................... Fanfares pour Tous les Temps
Ames, William...Composition
Anderson, Thomas ....Transitions
Andriessen, Jurriaan...Antifona e Fusione
Andriessen, Jurriaan..Concertino
Andriessen, Jurriaan... Entrata Festiva
Andriessen, Jurriaan..Hommage à Milhaud
Andriessen, Jurriaan.. Respiration-Suite
Antunes, Jorge...Intervertige
Arnell, Richard..Ceremonial and Flourish
Arnell, Richard.......................................Ceremonial and Flourish, Op. 43
Arnold, Malcolm .... Trevelyan Suite, Op. 96
Arrieu, Claude...Dixtuor
Asioli, Bonifazio...Serenade
Aubin, Tony..Cressida Fanfare
Autori, Franco..La Senese '70
Babbitt, Milton ....Composition for 12 Instruments
Babusek, František ....Noneto
Bäck, Sven-Erik...Chamber Symphony
Baervoets, Raymond ....Fanfare Héroique & Fanfare Joyeuse
Balada, Leonardo...Sonata for 10 Winds
Balassa, Sándor ....Xenia-Nonet
Ballou, Esther Williamson.. Suite for Winds
Barber, Samuel...Medea - Cave of the Heart
Barber, Samuel...Mutations from Bach
Bassett, Leslie ....Nonet
Bauer, Marion...Aquarelle Op. 39, No. 2
Bauer, Marion...Patterns, Op. 41, No. 2
Bauszern, Waldemar von..Chamber Symphony
Beach, Bruce ....Fanfare and Chorale
Beach, Bruce ....Five Intagli
Beadell, Robert..Introduction and Allegro
Beale, James .... Five Still Lifes, Op. 32
Beck, Conrad .... Concerto

Becker, Gunther ....Game for Nine
Beckhelm, Paul.. Tragic March
Bedford, David..Trona for 12
Benes, Jiri ....Preference
Bennett, Richard Rodney... Jazz Calendar
Bentzon, Niels Viggo...Chamber Concerto, Op. 52
Bentzon, Niels Viggo...Climate Changes, Op. 474
Bentzon, Niels Viggo...Sinfonia Concertante, Op. 100
Bentzon, Niels Viggo......................... Sonata for Twelve Instruments, Op. 257
Berger, Arthur..Chamber Music
Berkeley, Michael..Chamber Symphony
Bernard, Jean Emile.. Divertissement
Beversdorf, Samuel Thomas..Cathedral Music
Beyer, Howard..Suite for Brass Instruments
Bilik, Jerry ....Sonata for Brass
Binkerd, Gordon..Three Canzonas
Birtwistle, Harrison .... Tragoedia
Birtwistle, Harrison ....Verses for Ensembles
Bland, William... Sonics I, II, III
Blank, Allan... Paganini Caprice (XIV)
Blatter, Alfred..Suite
Blickhan, Charles Timothy...................................... Variations/Permutations
Bliss, Arthur..Fanfare for a Coming of Age
Bliss, Arthur... Fanfare for the Lord Mayor of London
Bliss, Arthur.......................................Fanfare, Homage to Shakespeare
Bliss, Arthur.. The Women of Yueh
Bloch, Ernest .... Four Episodes
Blum, Robert ....Musik
Boccherini, Luigi ....Ouverture à Grand Orchestre, Op. 43
Boedijn, Gerard.................5 Concertante Epigram-Schetsen, Op. 159
Boehm, Yohanan..Divertimento
Bogusławski, Edward..Intonazioni I
Böhner, Johann Ludwig ....Serenade
Bois, Rob du..Circle
Bolcom, William..Session IV
Bon, Willem Frederik .... Passacaglia in Blue
Bonneau, Paul... Fanfare
Bonsel, Adriaan .... Folkloristische Suite
Bonvin, Ludwig ....Romance, Op. 19a
Bořkovec, Pavel..Nonetto
Borstlap, Dick..Fanfare II
Borstlap, Dick..Over de Verandering
Bortolotti, Mauro ....Studio per Cummings No. 2
Börtz, Daniel ....Kammarmusik
Bottenberg, Wolfgang ....Variables
Bottje, Will Gay..Serenade
Boykan, Martin .... Concerto
Bozay, Attila ....Serie, Op. 19
Bozay, Attila ....Sorozat
Božič, Darijan............................... Concerto Grosso in F Major
Bozza, Eugène..Fanfare Héroique

Bozza, Eugène..Messe Solennelle de Ste. Cécile
Bozza, Eugène.. Overture pour une Cérémonie
Brandl, Johann ....Grande Serenade, Op. 7
Brauer, Max .... Pan
Brenta, Gaston... Fanfare
Brenta, Gaston..Fanfare Héroique
Bresgen, Cesar..Dorfmusikanten Op. 14
Bresgen, Cesar...Jagdkonzert
Bresgen, Cesar.. Kammerkonzert, Op. 6
Brian, William Havergal..Festival Fanfare
Britten, Benjamin..Sinfonietta, Op. 1
Brown, Earle..Pentathis
Brown, Jonathan Bruce .... Fragments
Brown, Newel..Chant and Jubilee
Brown, Rayner..Passacaglia With Fugues
Brugk, Hans Melchior....................................Suite für 10 Blechbläser, Op. 8
Brumby, Colin James .... Fanfare
Brün, Herbert..Gestures for Eleven
Bucchi, Thomas..Battaglia
Büchtger, Fritz... Concertino II
Buck, Ole .... Chamber Music I
Buck, Ole .... Chamber Music II
Burghäuser, Jarmil ....Old Czech Fanfares
Butting, Max... Hausmusik, Op. 119
Canning, Thomas ....Meditation for Strings
Canning, Thomas ....Rondo
Caplet, André ....Suite Persane
Cardon, Louis.. Deux Concertos, Op. 10
Casanova, André .... Serenata
Castillon de Saint-Victor, Alexis ....Allegretto
Caturla, Alejandro.. Bembe
Cazden, Norman .... Concerto for Ten Instruments
Cazden, Norman .... Six Definitions
Cervelló, Jorge ....Catalisis
Chance, Nancy...Darksong
Charbonnier, Janine..Systems
Chaun, František..Divertimento
Chávez, Carlos.. Energía
Chávez, Carlos...Xochipilli
Chemin-Petit, Hans....................................Suite, Dr. Johannes Faust
Childs, Barney.. Jack's New Bag
Chou, Wen-Chung .... Soliloquy
Chou, Wen-Chung ....Two Miniatures from T'Ang
Chou, Wen-Chung ....Yu Ko
Chou, Wen-Chung .... Yun
Ciglic, Zvonimir .... Absurdi
Clementi, Aldo ....Concertino in forma di Variazioni
Clementi, Aldo .... Intermezzo
Cobine, Albert..Vermont Suite
Constant, Marius.. Musique de Concert
Cooke, Arnold..Sinfonietta

Copland, Aaron...Appalachian Spring Suite
Copland, Aaron...Ceremonial Fanfare
Copland, Aaron............................... Fanfare for the Common Man
Copland, Aaron...Nonet
Corghi, Azio ....Actus I
Cossart, Leland A...Suite, Op. 19
Cowell, Henry ....Fanfare for the Forces of the Latin American Allies
Cowell, Henry ....Polyphonica
Crawford, John ....Three Palindromes
Creely, Robert ....Music for Ten Instruments
Crosse, Gordon .... Ariadne
Cunningham, Michael...Spring Sonnet
Custer, Arthur...Cycle for Nine Instruments
Davidovsky, Mario... Inflexions
Davidovsky, Mario...Noneto
Davies, Peter Maxwell...Eram Quasi Agnus
Davis, Anthony...Hemispheres
Davis, Anthony...Wayang IV
Delas, José Luis de .... Imago
Delden, Lex van... Fantasia, Op. 87
Delden, Lex van... Nonet, Op. 101
Delden, Lex van... Sinfonia No. 7
Denisov, Edison...Music
Devienne, Francois...Overture
Devresse, Godfroid .... Fanfare
Diamond, David...Elegy in Memory of Maurice Ravel
Diamond, David...Nonet
Diemente, Edward ....Love Song for Autumn
Ditters von Dittersdorf, Karl...Concertino
Dodge, Charles... Folia
Doležálek, Jan E...Twelve Ecossaises
Donatoni, Franco...Lied
Donatoni, Franco...Movimento
Donatoni, Franco...Solo per 10
Dondeyne, Désiré...Trois Esquesses de Fanfare
Druckman, Jacob...Incenters
DuBois, Robert ....Espace à Remplir Pour Onze Musiciens
Durey, Louis...Interlude
Dvořák, Antonin...Serenade, Op. 44
Dzierlatka, Arié...Melodies
Eckhardt, Sophie-Carmen ....Nonet
Edler, Robert... Reflections
Edwards, George .... Bits
Edwards, George .... Uroboros
Egk, Werner... Divertissement
Egk, Werner... Polonaise
Eichheim, Henry...Oriental Impressions
Eisler, Hanns...Nonett No. 1
Eisler, Hanns...Nonette 2
Eisler, Hanns...Ouvertüre Zu Einem Lustspiel
Eisma, Will...If . . .

Eller, Heino .... Camera Eye
Enesco, Georges .... Dixtuor
Erb, Donald .... Fanfare
Erb, Donald .... Sonneries
Erbse, Heimo .... Nonett, Op. 28
Erickson, Robert .... Chamber Concerto
Etler, Alvin .... Concerto
Farkas, Ferenc .... Kleine Turmmusik
Farrenc, Jeanne Louise .... Nonetto, Op. 38
Feld, Jindřich .... Kammersuite
Feldman, Morton .... 11 Instruments
Feldman, Morton .... Ixion
Feldman, Morton .... Madame Press Died Last Week at 90
Feldman, Morton .... Numbers
Feldman, Morton .... Projection 5
Fellagara, Vittorio .... Serenata
Ferrari, Luc .... Flashes
Ficher, Jacobo .... Dos Poemas, Op. 10, No. 16 & 42
Fisher, Stephen .... Music for Nine Instruments
Flagello, Nicholas .... Chorale and Episode
Flagello, Nicholas .... Concertino
Fleming, Robert .... Maritime Suite
Foerster, Josef .... Nonet
Fontyn, Jacqueline .... Pour Onze Archets
Françaix, Jean .... 7 Danses d'après Les Malheurs de Sophie
Françaix, Jean .... L'Heure Du Berger
Françaix, Jean .... Neuf Pièces Caractéristiques
Françaix, Jean .... Sérénade
Franco, Johan .... Fanfare
Franco, Johan .... The Pilgrim's Progress
Frankel, Ben .... Bagatelles, Op. 35
Freedman, Harry .... Tsolum Summer
Fritsch, Johannes .... Modulation II
Froundberg, Ivar .... en Vue de Roesnaes
Fundal, Karsten .... Hoquetus
Ganz, Rudolf .... Brassy Prelude, Op. 31, No. 1
Ganz, Rudolf .... Woody Scherzo for 13 Instruments
Geissler, Fritz .... Nonett
Geissler, Fritz .... Ode an eine Nachtigall
Gentilucci, Armando .... Fantasia No. 2
Gentilucci, Armando .... Rifrazioni per 10
Genzmer, Harold .... Nonett
Geraedts, Jaap .... Koraal-Fanfare
Gerhard, Roberto .... Hymnody
Gerhard, Roberto .... Hymnody
Gerhard, Roberto .... Leo
Gerhard, Roberto .... Nonet
Gerschefski, Edwin .... Prelude
Gibson, Jon Charles .... Melody IV
Giefer, Willy .... Pro-Kontra
Gilbert, Anthony .... Brighton Piece

Gilse, Jan van ....Nonet
Glass, Philip...Glassworks
Glazounov, Alexander..Fanfares
Godron, Hugo..Amabile-Suite
Goldman, Richard Franco...................................... Hymn for Brass Choir
Goodenough, Forrest...Fanfarce
Goossens, Eugene...Petite Symphonie
Górecki, Henryk Mikolaj..................................Genesis, Op. 19, No. 2
Górecki, Henryk Mikolaj.. Muzyczka 2
Görner, Hans-Georg .... Intrada et Hymnus, Op. 20
Gounod, Charles...Petite Symphonie
Gouvy, Louis...Petite Suite Gauloise, Op. 90
Grandert, Johann...Nonett
Grant, Parks ....Prelude and Dance, Op. 39
Grovlez, Gabriel.. Nocturne
Gudmundsen-Holmgreen, Pell...Two Improvisations
Guézec, Jean-Pierre.................................... Concert en 3 Parties
Guinjoàn, Juan ....Fragment
Hába, Alois .... Nonet No. 1, Op. 40
Haddad, Donald ....Fugue in D Minor
Hahn, Reynaldo ....La Bal de Béatrice D'Este
Hamilton, Iain .... Windflowers
Harbison, John ....Confinement
Hardin, Burton ....Regal Festival Music
Harper, Edward ....Ricercare
Harris, Russell.. 3 Three-Parts
Hartley, Walter... Double Concerto
Hartley, Walter.. Sinfonia No. 3
Hartmann, Emil ....Serenade, Op. 43
Hauer, Josef ....Dance Suite No. 1, Op. 70
Hauer, Josef ....Dance Suite No. 2, Op. 71
Haydn, Franz Joseph...................... Cassazione, No. 2 in G Major, Hob. II:G1
Haydn, Franz Joseph.....................Cassazione, No. 3 in G Major, Hob. II:9
Haydn, Franz Joseph...................... Divertissement No. 1 in F Major, Hob. II:20
Haydn, Franz Joseph........................... Divertissement No. 2 in F Major
Haydn, Franz Joseph..............Feldpartitur, Chorale St. Antoine, Hob. II:46
Haydn, Franz Joseph..............................Nocturne, No. 7 in C Major, Hob. II:31
Haydn, Franz Joseph..............................Notturno I in C Major, Hob. II:25
Haydn, Franz Joseph..Notturno II in C Major
Haydn, Franz Joseph............................Notturno II in F Major, Hob. II:26
Haydn, Franz Joseph............................Notturno V in C Major, Hob. II:29
Haydn, Franz Joseph................................... Partita in F Major
Haydn, Franz Joseph...................... Two Marches, Hob. VIII:1&2
Hazell, Chris.. 3 Brass Cats
Hazell, Chris..Kraken
Hazzard, Peter .... Mentor
Hechtel, Herbert... Trial
Hedwall, Lennart ....Partita
Heider, Werner..Sonatina
Hemel, Oscar van.. Divertimento No. 2
Henkemans, Hans...Primavera

Josephs, Wilfred...Concert a Dodici, Op. 21
Kahn, Erich.. Actus Tragicus
Kahn, Erich...Petite Suite Bretonne
Kahowez, Günter ....Bardo-Puls
Kanitz, Ernest ....Serenade
Kapr, Jan.. Omaggio Alla Tromba
Karel, Rudolf ....Nonetto
Karlins, Martin ....Concerto Grosso
Kee, Cornelis..Blijde Incomste
Ketting, Otto .... Intrada Festiva
Ketting, Otto .... Variazioni per Orchestra
Keuris, Tristan..Musica Concertante
Killmayer, Wilhelm ....Kindertage
Kirchner, Leon...Illuminations
Kirchner, Leon.. Music for Twelve
Kirnberger, Johann... Twelve Minuets
Kittl, Johann Friedrich ....Nonet
Klebanov, Demitri..Ukrainian Concertino
Kleinsinger, George.. Design for Woodwinds
Klughardt, August ....Nonetto
Klusák, Jan...Invention
Klusák, Jan.. Invention for Strings
Knight, Morris...Varieties for Brass
Knox, Charles... Symphony
Knox, Charles............................Symphony for Brass & Percussion
Knussen, Oliver..Ophelia Dances I, Op. 13A
Knussen, Oliver.. Pantomine
Kocscár, Miklós...Capricorn Concerto
Koetsier, Jan..Nonett
Koetsier, Jan...Rondo Sereno
Kohn, Karl...Impromptus
Kohn, Karl... The Prophet Bird
Kolb, Barbara .... Trobar Clus
Kopelent, Marek...............................A Few Minutes with an Oboist
Kox, Hans...Cyclofonie IV
Koželuh, Leopold ....Two Suites for Wind Nonet
Krenek, Ernst.................................Drei Lustige Märsche, Op. 44
Krenek, Ernst.. Marginal Sounds
Krenek, Ernst..........................Symphonic Music for 9 Solo Inst.
Krenek, Ernst.................Symphony Music in Two Movements, Op. 11
Kroeger, Karl................... The Firebugs Overture and Incidental Music
Krommer, Franz ....Concertante, Op. 38 and 39
Krommer, Franz .... Concertino, Op. 18
Krommer, Franz ....Nonet, Op. 79
Kubik, Gail..Divertimento No. 1
Kubin, Rudolf..Nonetto
Kučera, Václav.. Dramata
Kupferman, Meyer..Concertino
Kupferman, Meyer...Infinites 14
Kwiatkowski, Ryszard..Baltic Sonnets
Laderman, Ezra ....Cadence

Malipiero, Riccardo...Ricercari
Manzoni, Giacomo.......................................Parafrasi Con Finale
Manzoni, Giacomo..Spiel per 10
Marcus, Ada Belle Gross ....A Setting to Seasons
Maros, Rudolf.. Musica da Camera
Marteau, Henri...Sérénade, Op. 20
Marttinen, Tauno..Nonet
Mason, Benedict............ Imposing a Regular Pattern in Chaos and Heterophony
Mason, Benedict... The Hinterstoisser Traverse
Massenet, Jules ....Introduction & Variations, Op. 19
Masson, Gérard...Quest I
Matsudaira, Yoritsune... Serenata
Matsushita, Shin-Ichi............................... 5 Tempos for 11 Instruments
Matsushita, Shin-Ichi...........................Correlations for 3 Groups
Matthews, Colin ....Ceres
Matthews, William.....................................Letters from Home
Mayer, William .... Essay for Brass and Winds
Mazzinghi, Joseph ....Some Pieces in Harmony, Op. 33
McBeth, William Francis..Canticle
McCauley, William .... Five Miniatures
McKay, George Frederick ....Bravura Prelude
Merikanto, Aarre ....Nonetto
Meriläinen, Usko ....Partiti
Meulemans, Arthur .... Fanfare voor de Inauguratie van K.V.S.
Meyerowitz, Jan..Short Suite
Mica, František Adam......................................Concertino Notturno
Miereanu, Costin..Couleurs du Temps
Mikoda, Bořivoj.................................. Nonetto, Op. 30
Milhaud, Darius...Actualités
Milhaud, Darius...Dixtuor à cordes
Milhaud, Darius............................... Musique pour Graz
Milhaud, Darius...Printemps
Mills, Charles...Chamber Concerto
Mingus, Charles..Revelations
Miroglio, Francis...Espaces V
Miroglio, Francis...Réseaux
Mitrea-Celarianu, Mihai..Signaux
Molbe, Heinrich...Dezett, Op. 91
Molbe, Heinrich...Dezett, Op. 104
Molbe, Heinrich...Dezett, Op. 109
Molbe, Heinrich...Dezett, Op. 113
Molbe, Heinrich...Dezett, Op. 118
Molbe, Heinrich...Dezett, Op. 124
Molbe, Heinrich...Dezett, Op. 129
Molbe, Heinrich...Grüne Klänge, Op. 141
Molbe, Heinrich...Hymn De Printemps, Op. 31
Molbe, Heinrich...Intermezzo, Op. 81
Molbe, Heinrich...Intermezzo, Op. 110
Molbe, Heinrich...Intermezzo, Op. 111
Molbe, Heinrich...Nonet, Op. 26
Molbe, Heinrich...Nonet, Op. 61

Pablo, Luis de...Modulos I
Paccagnini, Angelo...................................... Musica da Camera
Pálsson, Páll... Crystals
Parchman, Gene...Fifth Symphony
Parris, Robert...Lamentations & Praises
Parris, Robert.. The Golden Net
Parry, Charles Hubert...Nonet, Op. 70
Pauer, Ernst...Divertimento
Paumgartner, Bernhard ....Divertimento
Payne, Anthony.....................................Fanfares and Processional
Peaslee, Richard...Divertimento
Peterson, Wayne ....Encounters
Petrescu, Dinu.. Musique
Petrić, Ivo.. Inlaid-Work
Petrić, Ivo.................................... Petit Concerto De Chambre
Petyrek, Felix... Arabische Suite
Phillips, Peter... Chimer
Piechowska, Alina..Imaginaire
Pisk, Paul.. Cortège, Op. 53B
Piston, Walter.......................................Ceremonial Fanfare
Piston, Walter.......................................Divertimento for Nine Inst.
Piston, Walter.. Fanfare
Pittaluga, Gustavo ....Petite Suite
Pleskow, Raoul......................................Movement for 9 Players
Polin, Claire.................................... The Journey of Owain Madoc
Pollock, Robert... Revolution
Ponse, Luctor.................................... Euterpe, Op. 37
Pospíšil, Jurraj ....Nonet No. 2
Pospíšil, Jurraj ....Trojversia, Op. 22
Post, Jennifer.. The Next Call
Poulenc, Francis.............................. Mouvements Perpétuels
Powell, Mel.. Modules
Praag, Henri C. Van ....Dixtuor
Praag, Henri C. Van ....Fantasie
Pragg, Henri C. Van ....Music
Premru, Raymond....................................Divertimento for Brass
Presser, William.............................. Passacaglia and Fugue
Presser, William..Research
Ramovš, Primož..Apel
Rasmussen, Karl Aage......................Movements on a Moving Line
Rawsthorne, Alan...............................Concerto for 10 Instruments
Read, Gardner............................ Chorale and Fughetta, Op. 83A
Read, Gardner.................... Sound Piece for Brass & Percussion, Op. 82
Reck, David .... Number 1 for 12 Performers
Reed, Alfred.. Double Wind Quintet
Reiner, Karel ....Kleine Suite
Reizenstein, Franz ....Serenade
Revueltas, Silvestre ....Homenaje a Federico García Lorca
Revueltas, Silvestre ....Planos, A Geometric Dance
Revueltas, Silvestre ....Three Sonnets
Reynolds, Roger .... Quick Are the Mouths of Earth

Vostřák, Zbynek...Tao
Vriend, Jan ....Paroesie
Vries, Klaas de .... Moeilijkheden
Wagner, Richard .... Siegfried Idyll
Wanek, Friedrich K. .... Vier Grotesken
Ward, William...Fantasia
Warren, Raymond.......................................Music for Harlequin
Washburn, Robert ....Concertino
Weber, Carl Maria von ....March for Harmonie
Webern, Anton von.................................Concerto, Op. 24
Webern, Anton von................................. Sinfonie, Op. 21
Welin, Karl-Erik.. NR 3
Werdin, Ebern.. Konzertante Musik
Werle, Lars Johan ....Summer Music
Whittenberg, Charles ....Variations for Nine
Wijdeveld, Wolfgang ....Concertpiece
Wilder, Alec.....................................A Debutante's Diary
Wiszniewski, Zbigniew............................. Chamber Music No. 4
Wolff, Christian..Nine
Wolpe, Stefan....................................Chamber Piece No. 1
Woollen, Russell ....Triptych, Op. 34
Wuorinen, Charles.......................................Canzona
Wuorinen, Charles.......................................Chamber Concerto
Wuorinen, Charles.......................................The Winds
Wyttenbach, Jürg..................................... Divisions
Xenakis, Iannis......................................Analogique A
Xenakis, Iannis......................................Atrées
Xenakis, Iannis......................................Linaia-Agon.
Xenakis, Iannis...................................... Phlegra
Xenakis, Iannis......................................ST/10-1,080262
Young, Lynden de .... Divertissement
Yttrehus, Rolv .... Music for Winds, Percussion & Viola
Zaninelli, Luigi...Jubilate Deo
Zaninelli, Luigi................................Music for a Solemn Occasion
Zimmermann, Gustav..................... Rheinische Kirmestänze
Zindars, Earl..The Brass Square
Zonn, Paul .... Canzonni, Overo Sonate Concertare Con-Serere
Zonn, Paul ....Sonorum I

4 Violins, 2 Violas, 2 Cellos, and Double Bass

Akutagawa, Yasushi................................ Music for Strings No. 1
Amato, Bruno ....Basses and Brass
Autori, Franco.......................................La Senese '70
Bäck, Sven-Erik....................................Chamber Symphony
Bauer, Marion....................................Aquarelle Op. 39, No. 2
Bauszern, Waldemar von.................................Chamber Symphony
Beckwith, John......................................Circle with Tangents
Benguerel, Xavier.. Consort Music

2 Violins, Viola, and Double Bass

Abrahamsen, Hans..Lied in Fall
Asioli, Bonifazio..Serenade
Aubéry, Prudent-Louis .... Grande Sérénade, Op. 48
Beck, Conrad .... Concerto
Cardon, Louis... Deux Concertos, Op. 10
Crawford, John ....Three Palindromes
Hasquenoph, Pierre... Divertissement
Michel, Joseph .... Serenata
Mozart, Wolfgang Amadeus... Serenade, K. 100
Mozart, Wolfgang Amadeus... Serenade, K. 320
Rosetti, Francesco Antonio... La Chasse
Rosetti, Francesco Antonio..Six Symphonies
Rosetti, Francesco Antonio..Three Symphonies, Op. 5
Rosetti, Francesco Antonio.. Two Symphonies, Op. 13
Seiffert, Max .... Serenata
Stamitz, Karl .... La Chasse
Stravinsky, Igor..Ragtime
Töeschi, Johann ....Three Symphonies, Op. 7
Werdin, Ebern... Konzertante Musik

Compositions Including
Woodwind Combinations

Flute, Oboe, Clarinet, Bassoon, and Horn

Abrahamsen, Hans..Lied in Fall
Abrahamsen, Hans..Märchenbilder
Adaskin, Murray...Rondino for Nine Instruments
Aitken, Hugh ....Serenade
Ames, William .... Composition
Andriessen, Jurriaan..Antifona e Fusione
Andriessen, Jurriaan..Rouw Past Elektra...
Angerer, Paul ....Cogitatio
Antoniou, Théodore .... Concertino, Op. 21
Antunes, Jorge...Intervertige
Apostel, Hans Erich................................... Fischerhaus-Serenade, Op. 45
Arnold, Malcolm ....Trevelyan Suite, Op. 96
Arrieu, Claude...Dixtuor
Babbitt, Milton ....Composition for 12 Instruments
Babusek, František ....Noneto
Baervoets, Raymond .... Musica per 14 Strumenti
Balada, Leonardo..Sonata for 10 Winds

Barber, Samuel...Medea - Cave of the Heart
Bassett, Leslie ....Nonet
Beethoven, Ludwig van ....March in C Major
Beethoven, Ludwig van ....Twelve Contra Dances
Bentzon, Niels Viggo................................Climate Changes, Op. 474
Bentzon, Niels Viggo...................... Sonata for Twelve Instruments, Op. 257
Berger, Arthur...Chamber Music
Bernard, Jean Emile.. Divertissement
Bialas, Günther...Partita
Bianchi, Gabriele.. Four Studi da Malu
Birtwistle, Harrison .... Tragoedia
Birtwistle, Harrison ....Verses for Ensembles
Blickhan, Charles Timothy........................... Variations/Permutations
Bloch, Ernest .... Four Episodes
Boedijn, Gerard...........................5 Concertante Epigram-Schetsen, Op. 159
Bonsel, Adriaan .... Folkloristische Suite
Bonvin, Ludwig ....Romance, Op. 19a
Bořkovec, Pavel..Nonetto
Bottje, Will Gay...Serenade
Boykan, Martin .... Concerto
Brautigam, Helmut..Nonet, Op. 11
Bresgen, Cesar..Jagdkonzert
Britten, Benjamin...Sinfonietta, Op. 1
Brün, Herbert..Gestures for Eleven
Brün, Herbert.. Passacaille, Op. 25
Bubak, Josef...Nonet, Op. 17
Buck, Ole .... Chamber Music I
Buck, Ole .... Chamber Music II
Bumcke, Gustav..Promenades, Op. 22
Busch, Adolf ....Divertimento
Castillon de Saint-Victor, Alexis ....Allegretto
Caturla, Alejandro.. Tres Danzas Cubanas
Cazden, Norman .... Concerto for Ten Instruments
Chaun, František..Divertimento
Cole, Hugo... Serenade for Nine Wind Instruments
Corghi, Azio ....Divertimento
Cowell, Henry .... Polyphonica
David, Thomas.....................................Concerto for 9 Instruments
Denisov, Edison...Music
Dobiáš, Václav .... O Rodne Zemi
Dost, Rudolf..La Bal de Béatrice D'Este
Druckman, Jacob..Incenters
Dubois, Théodore..Dixtuor
Eckhardt, Sophie-Carmen..Nonet
Egk, Werner.. Divertissement
Eisma, Will..If . . .
Erickson, Robert...Chamber Concerto
Escher, Rudolf...Sinfonia
Farrenc, Jeanne Louise....................................... Nonetto, Op. 38
Feld, Jindřich ....Kammersuite
Feld, Jindřich ....Nonetto, Suite de Chambre

Ficher, Jacobo	Dos Poemas, Op. 10, No. 16 & 42
Finke, Fedelio	Suite, Musik für 11 Bläser
Flegier, Ange	Dixtuor in F Minor
Flosman, Oldřich	Nonet No. 2
Foerster, Josef	Nonet
Folprecht, Zdeněk	Concertino, Op. 21
Françaix, Jean	L'Heure Du Berger
Françaix, Jean	Sérénade
Frankel, Ben	Bagatelles, Op. 35
Frid, Géza	Twelve Metamorphoses, Op. 54A
Gabichvadze, Revaz	Quick Motion
Geissler, Fritz	Nonett
Geissler, Fritz	Ode an eine Nachtigall
Gerhard, Roberto	Nonet
Giefer, Willy	Pro-Kontra
Giuranna, Bruno	Adagio e Allegro Da Concerto
Goossens, Eugene	Fantasy for Nine Wind Instruments
Goossens, Eugene	Petite Symphonie
Gounod, Charles	Petite Symphonie
Gouvy, Louis	Petite Suite Gauloise, Op. 90
Grabner, Hermann	Perkeo Suite for Wind Orch., Op. 15
Grandert, Johann	Nonett
Grimm, Carl Hugo	Byzantine Suite
Grovlez, Gabriel	Nocturne
Gruber, Heinz	Revue for 10 Instruments
Gwilt, David	Suite for Woodwind & Brass Instruments
Hába, Alois	Nonet No. 1, Op. 40
Hába, Alois	Nonet No. 3, Op. 82
Hahn, Reynaldo	La Bal de Béatrice D'Este
Harris, Donald	Ludus I
Harris, Donald	Ludus, Chamber Concerto
Harsányi, Tibor	Nonett
Hartley, Walter	Double Concerto
Hartmann, Emil	Serenade, Op. 43
Hasquenoph, Pierre	Divertissement
Hasquenoph, Pierre	Divertissement pour Dixtuor
Hess, Willy	Serenade, Op. 19
Hiller, Lejaren	Divertimento
Hindemith, Paul	Concert Music, Op. 36, No. 1
Hindemith, Paul	Kammermusik No. 3
Hlobil, Emil	Nonet, Op. 27
Hoch, Francesco	L'Oggetto Disincantato
Holloway, Robin	Divertimento
Honegger, Arthur	Pastorale d'Eté
Horvath, Josef	Sothis I
Hovhaness, Alan	Tower Music, Op. 129
Hovland, Egil	Music for Ten Instruments, Op. 28
Huggler, John	Music for 13 Instruments, Op. 75
Huse, Peter	Objects
Ippolitov-Ivanov, Mikhail	Caucasian Sketches, Dans la Mosque
Ives, Charles	Symphony No. 3 - The Camp Meeting

Jacob, Gordon.. Diversions
Janáček, Leoš...Mala Suite
Jaroch, Jiří .... Detska Suita
Jaroch, Jiří .... Kindersuite
Jaroch, Jiří .... Nonetto II
Jolas, Betsy..J.D.E.
Josephs, Wilfred..Concert a Dodici, Op. 21
Kahn, Erich... Actus Tragicus
Kahn, Erich...Petite Suite Bretonne
Kalabis, Viktor.. Klasicky Nonet
Kanitz, Ernest ....Serenade
Karlins, Martin ....Concerto Grosso
Kelterborn, Rudolf ....Musik
Ketting, Otto .... Variazioni per Orchestra
Kirchner, Leon.. Music for Twelve
Kleinsinger, George...Design for Woodwinds
Klingler, Karl... Variations in A Major
Klusák, Jan..Invention
Knussen, Oliver.. Pantomine
Kopelent, Marek..................................... Pocta Vladimiru Holanovi
Kox, Hans... Cyclofony VIII
Kubik, Gail..Divertimento No. 1
Kubin, Rudolf..Nonetto
Kubizek, Augustin.. Quartetto da Camera, Op. 24a
Kubizek, Augustin.. Sinfonia da Camera, Op. 26b
Kwiatkowski, Ryszard..Baltic Sonnets
Lalo, Edouard.. Morning Serenade
Lampe, Walther..Serenade, Op. 7
Landré, Guillaume .... Sonata Festiva
Lange, Gustav.. Nonet in F Major
Lauber, Joseph.....................................Serenade for 14 Wind Instruments
Leibowitz, René ....Chamber Concerto, Op. 10
Leibowitz, René ....Chamber Symphony, Op. 16
Leibowitz, René ....Suite, Op. 81
Leichtling, Alan...Item 72-D
Leitermeyer, Fritz...Divertimento, Op. 53
Leleu, Jeanne...Suite Symphonique
Lessard, John ....Concerto for Wind Instruments
Lewis, Anthony... Pieces of Eight
Lewis, Peter... Lamentation, 3 Epigrams
Lieberson, Peter ....Wind Messengers
Luigini, Alexandre...Aubade, Op. 13
Lutoslawski, Witold.. Slides
Lutyens, Elizabeth ....Six Tempi
Macchi, Egisto.. Composizione 3
Maksymiuk, Jerzy...Decet
Malipiero, Gian...Serenata Mattutina
Malipiero, Riccardo.. Mosaico
Malipiero, Riccardo...Ricercari
Martinů, Bohuslav ....Nonetto
Marttinen, Tauno..Nonet

Mason, Benedict... The Hinterstoisser Traverse
Maštalíř, Jaroslav..Nonetto
Mayer, William .... Essay for Brass and Winds
McCauley, William .... Five Miniatures
Méfano, Paul... Interferences
Meriläinen, Usko ....Impression
Mikoda, Bořivoj.. Nonetto, Op. 30
Milhaud, Darius.. Musique pour Graz
Mills, Charles..Chamber Concerto
Montsalvatge, Bassols Xavier ....5 Invocaciones al Crucificado
Moór, Emanuel...Dixtuor, Op. 103
Moór, Emanuel.. Suite, Op. 103
Nagel, Robert ....Divertimento
Nono, Luigi..Canti per 13
Novák, Jan .... Baletti a 9
Nunes, Emanuel.. Dawn Wo
Odstrčil, Karel .... Siluety
Onslow, George .... Nonetto, Op. 77
Osterc, Slavko ....Nonet
Otten, Ludwig...Divertimento
Pálsson, Páll... Crystals
Parris, Robert... The Golden Net
Parry, Charles Hubert...Nonet, Op. 70
Pauer, Ernst..Divertimento
Perilhou, Albert... Divertissement
Persichetti, Vincent...Serenade No. 1
Petrić, Ivo................................... Divertimento for Slavko Osterc
Petyrek, Felix... Arabische Suite
Pierné, Gabriel...March of Little Fauns
Ponse, Luctor.. Euterpe, Op. 37
Post, Jennifer...The Next Call
Poulenc, Francis...Mouvements Perpétuels
Powell, Mel.. Modules
Praag, Henri C. Van ....Dixtuor
Praag, Henri C. Van ....Fantasie
Pragg, Henri C. Van ....Music
Pratella, Francesco ....Per un Dramma Orientale, Op. 40
Rasmussen, Karl Aage..........................Movements on a Moving Line
Reed, Alfred.. Double Wind Quintet
Reiner, Karel ....Kleine Suite
Rheinberger, Joseph... Nonet, Op. 139
Řídký, Jaroslav ....Nonett, Op. 32
Rieti, Vittorio .... Madrigal in Four Movements
Rochberg, George.............................Music for the Magic Theater
Rosetti, Francesco Antonio .... Partita in F
Rowland, David... Tropisms
Ruders, Poul.....................................4 Dances in 1 Movement
Ruders, Poul .... Nightshade
Rudziński, Witold ....Nonet
Rychlik, Józef ....Africky Cyklus

Saint-Saëns, Camille..Deuxième Suite
Samazeuilh, Gustave.....................................Divertissement and Musette
Santoro, Claudio ....Intermitencias II
Saxton, Robert ....Double Quintet
Schildknecht, Bjorn ....Fugerat Forspel
Schoeck, Othmar..Serenade, Op. 1
Schoenberg, Arnold..Chamber Symphony, Op. 9
Scholz, Richard ....Second Divertimento for 9 Winds
Schreck, Gustav...Nonett, Op. 40
Schudel, Thomas ....Set No. 2
Schuller, Gunther...Double Quintet
Schuman, William..Night Journey
Schwartz, Elliott......................................Concert Piece for Ten Players
Sciarino, Salvatore... Da un Divertimento
Searle, Humphrey.. Sinfonietta, Op. 49
Searle, Humphrey................................ Variations and Finale, Op. 34
Sekles, Bernhard ....Serenade, Op. 14
Siqueira, José de Lima ....Pregao for Eleven Instruments
Sixta, Jozef ....Noneto
Skalkottas, Nikos......................................Andante Sostenuto
Škvor, František ....Nonet II Prazsky
Škvor, František .... Nonetto in B Minor
Sørensen, Bent... Clairobscur
Sørensen, Bent... Shadowland
Southers, Leroy, Jr. ....Concert Piece
Spohr, Ludwig.....................................Nonet in F, Op. 31
Šrom, Karel.. Märchen
Stearns, Peter...Serenade
Stewart, Robert...Two Ricercari
Strauss, Richard...Serenade, Op. 7
Strauss, Richard...Suite, Op. 4
Stravinsky, Igor.............................. Eight Instrumental Miniatures
Stravinsky, Igor.............................. Song of Hauleurs on the Volga
Striegler, Kurt......................................Kammer-Sinfonie, Op. 14
Striegler, Kurt..Nonet, Op. 14
Sutermeister, Heinrich..................Modeste Mignon Nach Einem Walzer
Szymanski, Pawel...............................Quasi una Sinfonietta
Taraba, Bohuslav....................................Three Meditations
Tcherepnin, Nikolai.......................................Sonatine, Op. 61
Thomsen, Geraldine...Nonett
Tomasi, Henri-Frédien ....Jeux de Geishas
Turner, Robert ....Variations and Toccata
Van der Velden, Renier..Etude
Van der Velden, Renier..Les Ancêtres
Vaughan Williams, Ralph.............................. Scherzo alla Marcia
Verrall, John..Nonette
Vlad, Roman.. Serenata
Vogt, Hans...Concertino
Volans, Kevin.. Chevron
Vomáčka, Boleslav..Nonett
Wagner, Richard .... Siegfried Idyll

Washburn, Robert ....Concertino
Weber, Carl Maria von ....March for Harmonie
Whittenberg, Charles ....Variations for Nine
Wijdeveld, Wolfgang ....Concertpiece
Wiszniewski, Zbigniew...............................Chamber Music No. 4
Wolf-Ferrari, Ermanno ....Kammersymphonie, Op. 8
Xenakis, Iannis...Phlegra
Zillig, Winfried..Serenade No. 4

2 Flutes, 2 Oboes, 2 Clarinets, 2 Bassoons, and 2 Horns

Andriessen, Jurriaan...Concertino
Andriessen, Jurriaan...Respiration-Suite
Angerer, Paul...Musica Articolata
Arnell, Richard...Serenade, Op. 57
Ballou, Esther Williamson..................................Suite for Winds
Bauer, Marion.................................Aquarelle Op. 39, No. 2
Bauer, Marion.................................Patterns, Op. 41, No. 2
Bernard, Jean Emile.............................Divertissement, Op. 36
Boehm, Yohanan..Divertimento
Bon, Willem Frederik ....Passacaglia in Blue
Brauer, Max ....Pan
Caplet, André ....Suite Persane
Clementi, Aldo ....Intermezzo
Corghi, Azio ....Actus I
Cossart, Leland A...Suite
Cossart, Leland A..Suite, Op. 19
Delden, Lex van ....Sinfonia No. 7
Enesco, Georges...Dixtuor
Erod, Ivan..Capriccio
Françaix, Jean..............7 Danses d'après Les Malheurs de Sophie
Françaix, Jean................................Neuf Pièces Caractéristiques
Hedwall, Lennart ....Partita
Hemel, Oscar van...Divertimento No. 2
Hess, Willy..Suite, Op. 53
Jacob, Gordon........................More Old Wine in New Bottles
Jacob, Gordon........................Old Wine in New Bottles
Jaeger, David..........................Double Woodwind Quintet
Lenot, Jacques...Comme au Loin
Lewis, Peter..Sestina
Lilien, Ignace..................................Sonatine Apollinique
Lutyens, Elizabeth ....Music for Wind
Melin, Bengt...Menuet Badin
Moyse, Louis..Divertimento
Pablo, Luis de...Credo
Pauer, Jiří ....Musica da Concerto
Raff, Joseph Joachim ....Sinfonietta, Op. 188
Sporck, Georges..............................Landscapes of Normandy
Stringham, Edwin ....Nocturne

Taneyev, Alexander.............................Andante for Double Woodwind Quintet
Vranicky, Pavel .... Jägermärsche
Wanek, Friedrich K. .... Vier Grotesken
Zimmermann, Gustav...Rheinische Kirmestänze

Flute, Oboe, Clarinet, and Bassoon

Adler, Samuel.. Music for Eleven
Andriessen, Jurriaan....................................Hommage à Milhaud
Baksa, Robert ....Nonet
Bedford, David...Trona for 12
Bliss, Arthur.. The Women of Yueh
Bottenberg, Wolfgang ....Variables
Brown, Rayner....................................Passacaglia With Fugues
Caturla, Alejandro.. Bembe
Cervelló, Jorge ....Catalisis
Davidovsky, Mario...Noneto
Dubois, Théodore..Nonetto
Ebenhoh, Horst............................... 4 Scenes for 10, Op. 21, No. 1
Edwards, George .... Bits
Fleming, Robert...Maritime Suite
Franco, Johan ....The Pilgrim's Progress
Frankel, Ben....................................Bagatelles (Cinque Pezzi Notturni)
Ganz, Rudolf.................................. Woody Scherzo for 13 Instruments
Guézec, Jean-Pierre....................................... Concert en 3 Parties
Guinjoàn, Juan ....Fragment
Hauer, Josef ....Dance Suite No. 1, Op. 70
Hauer, Josef ....Dance Suite No. 2, Op. 71
Hauer, Josef ....Zwölftonspiel
Hindemith, Paul...Kammermusik, Op. 3
Holbrooke, Josef.. Nocturne
Ibert, Jacques...Capriccio
Klughardt, August ....Nonetto
Krenek, Ernst...........................Symphony Music in Two Movements, Op. 11
Kurka, Robert........................... The Good Soldier Schweik Polka and Waltz
Linn, Robert ....Concertino
Loeb, David..Partita da Camera
Lorentzen, Bent..Wunderblumen
Maes, Jef ....De Verloofden
Marteau, Henri...Sérénade, Op. 20
Massenet, Jules ....Introduction & Variations, Op. 19
Milhaud, Darius.. Aspen Serenade
Miroglio, Francis...Espaces V
Nilsson, Bo .... Zeitpunkte
Piston, Walter..Divertimento for Nine Inst.
Reizenstein, Franz ....Serenade
Salviucci, Giovanni.. Serenata
Schibler, Armin ....Prologue
Schibler, Armin .... Signal, Beschwörung

Schönherr, Max ....Dance
Sheriff, Noam ....Music
Stravinsky, Igor................................Concertino for 12 Instruments
Stürmer, Bruno ....Suite in G Minor, Op. 9
Taub, Bruce ....Chamber Variations 4
Tcherepnin, Ivan...Wheelwinds
Trimble, Lester...Concerto
Urbanner, Erich..Improvisation III
Vostřák, Zbynek..Tao
Wilder, Alec...A Debutante's Diary
Wuorinen, Charles...Canzona

Compositions Including
Brass Combinations

4 Trumpets, 4 Horns, 3 Trombones, and Tuba

Beach, Bruce ....Five Intagli
Beckhelm, Paul... Tragic March
Brian, William Havergal..Festival Fanfare
Copland, Aaron.. Fanfare for the Common Man
Durey, Louis..Interlude
Erb, Donald..Sonneries
Freed, Isadore..Symphony No. 2
Goldman, Richard Franco.. Hymn for Brass Choir
Huybrechts, Lode.. Divertissement
Jenni, Donald ....Allegro
Meriläinen, Usko ....Partiti
Read, Gardner..Chorale and Fughetta, Op. 83A
Shulman, Alan .... Top Brass, 6 Minutes for 12
Uber, David... Evolution I
Uber, David............................Twentieth Century Antiphonal, Op. 38
Young, Lynden de .... Divertissement
Zádor, Eugen..Suite
Zindars, Earl...The Brass Square

3 Trumpets, 4 Horns, 3 Trombones, and Tuba

Aubin, Tony...Cressida Fanfare
Aubin, Tony...Vitrail
Baervoets, Raymond ....Fanfare Héroique & Fanfare Joyeuse
Barber, Samuel...Mutations from Bach
Beversdorf, Samuel Thomas..Cathedral Music
Blank, Allan... Paganini Caprice (XIV)
Bliss, Arthur...Fanfare for a Coming of Age
Bliss, Arthur... Fanfare for the Lord Mayor of London
Bozza, Eugène...Fanfare Héroique
Bozza, Eugène.....................................Messe Solennelle de Ste. Cécile
Brenta, Gaston.. Fanfare
Brenta, Gaston..Fanfare Héroique
Brumby, Colin James .... Fanfare
Copland, Aaron..Ceremonial Fanfare
Devresse, Godfroid .... Fanfare
Diamond, David...............................Elegy in Memory of Maurice Ravel
Dukas, Paul .... Fanfare (La Peri)
Ganz, Rudolf.....................................Brassy Prelude, Op. 31, No. 1
Geraedts, Jaap...Koraal-Fanfare
Goodenough, Forrest..Fanfarce
Grant, Parks ....Prelude and Dance, Op. 39
Hardin, Burton .... Regal Festival Music
Husa, Karel.. Fanfare
Jacob, Gordon...Salute to U.S.A.
Jenni, Donald .... Allegro
Jongen, Joseph.. Fanfare Héroique, Op. 110
Knight, Morris..Varieties for Brass
Knox, Charles... Symphony
Knox, Charles..Symphony for Brass & Percussion
Lees, Benjamin..Fanfare for a Centennial
Louel, Jean..Fanfare J.M.
Louel, Jean...Fanfares
Meulemans, Arthur ....Fanfare voor de Inauguratie van K.V.S.
Moulaert, Raymond...Fanfares
Nelhybel, Vaclav..Designs for Brass
Niblock, James...Triptych for Brass
Parris, Herman..Four Rhapsodies
Piston, Walter.. Fanfare
Presser, William... Passacaglia and Fugue
Reynolds, Verne ....Prelude and Allegro
Rosseau, Norbert...Fanfare, Op. 58
Schmitt, Franz.......................................Fanfare, Le Camp de Pompée, Op. 69
Starer, Robert...Serenade for Brass
Taylor, Clifford..Inscriptions in Brass
Tcherepnin, Nikolai... Fanfare
Van der Velden, Renier... Fanfare
Ward, William...Fantasia

3 Trumpets, 3 Horns, and 3 Trombones

Adler, Samuel...Divertimento
Arnell, Richard..Ceremonial and Flourish
Beadell, Robert...Introduction and Allegro
Binkerd, Gordon...Three Canzonas
Boeck, August de.. Fanfare
Brugk, Hans Melchior.......................................Suite für 10 Blechbläser, Op. 8
Franco, Johan .... Fanfare
Görner, Hans-Georg .... Intrada et Hymnus, Op. 20
Haddad, Donald ....Fugue in D Minor
Hibbard, William .... Variations for Brass Nonet
Hogg, Merle.. Concerto
Lebow, Leonard ....Suite for Brass
Luening, Otto .... Fanfare for a Festive Occasion
Mailman, Martin..Two Fanfares, Op. 49
Nelhybel, Vaclav.. Slavic March
Novy, Donald..Sonatina
Presser, William..Research
Reynolds, Verne ....Theme and Variations
Vernon, W. Knight ....Suite

2 Trumpets, Horn, Trombone, and Tuba

Bennett, Richard Rodney.. Jazz Calendar
Finke, Fedelio... Suite, Musik für 11 Bläser
Krenek, Ernst..Drei Lustige Märsche, Op. 44
Mayer, William .... Essay for Brass and Winds
McCauley, William .... Five Miniatures
Nagel, Robert ....Divertimento
Reed, Alfred.. Double Wind Quintet
Saxton, Robert ....Double Quintet
Schifrin, Lalo .... Ritual of Sound
Schudel, Thomas .... Set No. 2
Schuller, Gunther...Double Quintet
Sear, Walter...Antiphony
Washburn, Robert ....Concertino

Compositions Including
Double Combinations

Flute, Oboe, Clarinet, Bassoon, Horn,
2 Violins, Viola, Cello, and Double Bass

Abrahamsen, Hans...Märchenbilder
Aitken, Hugh ....Serenade
Ames, William...Composition
Angerer, Paul..Cogitatio
Apostel, Hans Erich.....................................Fischerhaus-Serenade, Op. 45
Barber, Samuel..................................... Medea - Cave of the Heart
Berger, Arthur..Chamber Music
Bialas, Günther..Pastorale and Rondo
Bloch, Ernest .... Four Episodes
Bottje, Will Gay...Serenade
Britten, Benjamin.......................................Sinfonietta, Op. 1
Bubak, Josef...Nonet, Op. 17
Buck, Ole .... Chamber Music I
Buck, Ole .... Chamber Music II
Castillon de Saint-Victor, Alexis ....Allegretto
Cooke, Arnold...Sinfonietta
Cowell, Henry ....Polyphonica
Dubois, Théodore ....Dixtuor
Eisma, Will...If . . .
Escher, Rudolf...Sinfonia
Ficher, Jacobo.............................Dos Poemas, Op. 10, No. 16 & 42
Flegier, Ange...Dixtuor in F Minor
Françaix, Jean...Sérénade
Frankel, Ben...Bagatelles, Op. 35
Fundal, Kartsten ....Hoquetus
Grimm, Carl Hugo .... Byzantine Suite
Harris, Donald...Ludus I
Harris, Donald...............................Ludus, Chamber Concerto
Hasquenoph, Pierre........................... Divertissement pour Dixtuor
Henze, Hans Werner....................... In Memoriam Die Weisse Rose
Honegger, Arthur..Pastorale d'Eté
Horvath, Josef.. Sothis I
Hovland, Egil....................Music for Ten Instruments, Op. 28
Ives, Charles...................Symphony No. 3 - The Camp Meeting
Jacob, Gordon... Diversions
Jolas, Betsy...J.D.E.
Kahn, Erich...................................... Actus Tragicus
Klingler, Karl............................. Variations in A Major
Lalo, Edouard....................................... Morning Serenade
Landré, Guillaume .... Sonata Festiva
Lendvai, Erno...................................... Kammersuite, Op. 32
Malipiero, Riccardo .... Mosaico

Moór, Emanuel..Dixtuor, Op. 103
Moór, Emanuel.. Suite, Op. 103
Petrić, Ivo.. Divertimento for Slavko Osterc
Pierné, Gabriel...March of Little Fauns
Praag, Henri C. Van ....Dixtuor
Pratella, Francesco ....Per un Dramma Orientale, Op. 40
Rasmussen, Karl Aage..Movements on a Moving Line
Rawsthorne, Alan..Concerto for 10 Instruments
Rochberg, George..Music for the Magic Theater
Ruders, Poul..4 Dances in 1 Movement
Searle, Humphrey...Variations and Finale, Op. 34
Sekles, Bernhard ....Serenade, Op. 14
Siqueira, José de Lima ....Pregao for Eleven Instruments
Sørensen, Bent... Clairobscur
Sørensen, Bent... Shadowland
Southers, Leroy, Jr. ....Concert Piece
Striegler, Kurt...Kammer-Sinfonie, Op. 14
Szymanski, Pawel...Quasi una Sinfonietta
Tisne, Antoine ....Caractères
Turner, Robert ....Variations and Toccata
Wagner, Richard .... Siegfried Idyll
Zillig, Winfried..Serenade No. 4

Flute, Oboe, Clarinet, Bassoon, Horn, Violin, Viola, Cello, and Double Bass

Babbitt, Milton ....Composition for 12 Instruments
Babusek, František ....Noneto
Baervoets, Raymond .... Musica per 14 Strumenti
Bentzon, Niels Viggo......................... Sonata for Twelve Instruments, Op. 257
Bořkovec, Pavel...Nonetto
Boykan, Martin .... Concerto
Corghi, Azio ....Divertimento
David, Thomas......................................Concerto for 9 Instruments
Dobiáš, Václav ....O Rodne Zemi
Druckman, Jacob...Incenters
Eckhardt, Sophie-Carmen..Nonet
Erickson, Robert..Chamber Concerto
Farrenc, Jeanne Louise.. Nonetto, Op. 38
Feld, Jindřich ....Kammersuite
Feld, Jindřich ....Nonetto, Suite de Chambre
Flosman, Oldřich...Nonet No. 2
Foerster, Josef..Nonet
Folprecht, Zdeněk .... Concertino, Op. 21
Geissler, Fritz...Nonett
Giefer, Willy ....Pro-Kontra
Giuranna, Bruno.................................Adagio e Allegro Da Concerto
Hába, Alois .... Nonet No. 1, Op. 40

Hába, Alois	Nonet No. 3, Op. 82
Hindemith, Paul	Concert Music, Op. 36, No. 1
Hlobil, Emil	Nonet, Op. 27
Hoch, Francesco	L'Oggetto Disincantato
Jaroch, Jiří	Detska Suita
Jaroch, Jiří	Kindersuite
Jaroch, Jiří	Nonetto II
Kalabis, Viktor	Klasicky Nonet
Karel, Rudolf	Nonetto
Kirchner, Leon	Music for Twelve
Klusák, Jan	Invention
Kopelent, Marek	Pocta Vladimiru Holanovi
Kox, Hans	Cyclofony VIII
Kubik, Gail	Divertimento No. 1
Kubin, Rudolf	Nonetto
Kubizek, Augustin	Quartetto da Camera, Op. 24a
Kubizek, Augustin	Sinfonia da Camera, Op. 26b
Leibowitz, René	Chamber Concerto, Op. 10
Leibowitz, René	Chamber Symphony, Op. 16
Leibowitz, René	Suite, Op. 81
Lutoslawski, Witold	Slides
Martinů, Bohuslav	Nonetto
Marttinen, Tauno	Nonet
Maštalíř, Jaroslav	Nonetto
Mikoda, Bořivoj	Nonetto, Op. 30
Milhaud, Darius	Musique pour Graz
Nono, Luigi	Canti per 13
Novák, Jan	Baletti a 9
Odstrčil, Karel	Siluety
Onslow, George	Nonetto, Op. 77
Pauer, Ernst	Divertimento
Poulenc, Francis	Mouvements Perpétuels
Powell, Mel	Modules
Rheinberger, Joseph	Nonet, Op. 139
Řídký, Jaroslav	Nonett, Op. 32
Rudziński, Witold	Nonet
Santoro, Claudio	Intermitencias II
Schwartz, Elliott	Concert Piece for Ten Players
Searle, Humphrey	Sinfonietta, Op. 49
Škvor, František	Nonet II Prazsky
Škvor, František	Nonetto in B Minor
Spohr, Ludwig	Nonet in F, Op. 31
Šrom, Karel	Märchen
Thomsen, Geraldine	Nonett
Wiszniewski, Zbigniew	Chamber Music No. 4
Xenakis, Iannis	Phlegra

Flute, Oboe, Clarinet, Bassoon, Horn, 2 Violins, Viola, and Cello

Adaskin, Murray..Rondino for Nine Instruments
Antunes, Jorge...Intervertige
Bentzon, Niels Viggo..................................Climate Changes, Op. 474
Birtwistle, Harrison .... Tragoedia
Busch, Adolf ....Divertimento
Gabichvadze, Revaz ....Quick Motion
Geissler, Fritz..Ode an eine Nachtigall
Harsányi, Tibor ....Nonett
Hess, Willy...Serenade, Op. 19
Knussen, Oliver.. Pantomine
Lewis, Peter.. Lamentation, 3 Epigrams
Maksymiuk, Jerzy...Decet
Mills, Charles...Chamber Concerto
Pálsson, Páll .... Crystals
Rieti, Vittorio .... Madrigal in Four Movements
Samazeuilh, Gustave.............................Divertissement and Musette
Schoeck, Othmar..Serenade, Op. 1
Schoenberg, Arnold...........................Chamber Symphony, Op. 9
Sixta, Jozef ....Noneto
Stewart, Robert..Two Ricercari
Striegler, Kurt...Nonet, Op. 14
Taraba, Bohuslav...Three Meditations
Tomasi, Henri-Frédien ....Jeux de Geishas
Verrall, John...Nonette
Volans, Kevin.. Chevron
Wolf-Ferrari, Ermanno ....Kammersymphonie, Op. 8

Flute, Oboe, Clarinet, Bassoon, 2 Violins, Viola, Cello, and Double Bass

Baksa, Robert ....Nonet
Bliss, Arthur...The Women of Yueh
Bottenberg, Wolfgang ....Variables
Cervelló, Jorge ....Catalisis
Davidovsky, Mario..Noneto
Dubois, Théodore..Nonetto
Ebenhoh, Horst................................ 4 Scenes for 10, Op. 21, No. 1
Frankel, Ben.............................Bagatelles (Cinque Pezzi Notturni)
Guézec, Jean-Pierre.............................. Concert en 3 Parties
Klughardt, August ....Nonetto
Krenek, Ernst.............................Symphonic Music for 9 Solo Inst.
Krenek, Ernst.............................Symphony Music in Two Movements, Op. 11
Lorentzen, Bent...Wunderblumen
Massenet, Jules ....Introduction & Variations, Op. 19
Miroglio, Francis...Espaces V

Piston, Walter...Divertimento for Nine Inst.
Stürmer, Bruno ....Suite in G Minor, Op. 9
Trimble, Lester.. Concerto
Urbanner, Erich..Improvisation III

Flute, Oboe, Clarinet, Bassoon, 2 Violins, Viola, and Cello

Bedford, David...Trona for 12
Caturla, Alejandro.. Bembe
Fleming, Robert...Maritime Suite
Guinjoàn, Juan ....Fragment
Hauer, Josef ....Dance Suite No. 1, Op. 70
Hauer, Josef ....Dance Suite No. 2, Op. 71
Hauer, Josef ....Zwölftonspiel
Ibert, Jacques...Capriccio
Salviucci, Giovanni.. Serenata
Williams, Evans ....Fant'sy II

Flute, Oboe, Clarinet, Bassoon, Violin, Viola, Cello, and Double Bass

Edwards, George .... Bits
Loeb, David...Partita da Camera
Maes, Jef ....De Verloofden
Milhaud, Darius.. Aspen Serenade
Taub, Bruce .... Chamber Variations 4
Vostřák, Zbynek...Tao
Wuorinen, Charles..Canzona

Flute, Oboe, Clarinet, Bassoon, 2 Horns, 2 Trumpets, Trombone, and Tuba

Adaskin, Murray...Rondino for Nine Instruments
Antunes, Jorge.. Intervertige
Bentzon, Niels Viggo...Climate Changes, Op. 474
Birtwistle, Harrison .... Tragoedia
Busch, Adolf ....Divertimento
Gabichvadze, Revaz ....Quick Motion
Geissler, Fritz...Ode an eine Nachtigall
Harsányi, Tibor ....Nonett
Hess, Willy...Serenade, Op. 19
Knussen, Oliver .... Pantomine

Lewis, Peter... Lamentation, 3 Epigrams
Maksymiuk, Jerzy...Decet
Mills, Charles..Chamber Concerto
Pálsson, Páll... Crystals
Rieti, Vittorio .... Madrigal in Four Movements
Samazeuilh, Gustave..Divertissement and Musette
Schoeck, Othmar...Serenade, Op. 1
Schoenberg, Arnold..Chamber Symphony, Op. 9
Sixta, Jozef ....Noneto
Stewart, Robert...Two Ricercari
Striegler, Kurt...Nonet, Op. 14
Taraba, Bohuslav..Three Meditations
Tomasi, Henri-Frédien ....Jeux de Geishas
Verrall, John..Nonette
Volans, Kevin.. Chevron
Wolf-Ferrari, Ermanno .... Kammersymphonie, Op. 8

Compositions Including Harp

Arrigo, Girolamo...Fluxus, Op. 7
Babbitt, Milton ....Composition for 12 Instruments
Baervoets, Raymond .... Musica per 14 Strumenti
Balassa, Sándor...Xenia-Nonet
Bax, Arnold..Nonett
Beale, James .... Five Still Lifes, Op. 32
Benes, Jiri ....Preference
Berger, Arthur...Chamber Music
Birtwistle, Harrison .... Tragoedia
Boesmans, Philippe...Explosives
Bolcom, William...Session IV
Boykan, Martin .... Concerto
Brown, Earle..Pentathis
Bumcke, Gustav...Promenades, Op. 22
Cardon, Louis.. Deux Concertos, Op. 10
Casanova, André .... Serenata
Chance, Nancy..Darksong
Chevreville, Raymond ....Divertissement, Op. 40
Chou, Wen-Chung ....Two Miniatures from T'Ang
Cordero, Roque...Paz-Paiz-Peace
Cossart, Leland A...Suite, Op. 19
Creely, Robert ....Music for Ten Instruments
Davies, Peter Maxwell...Eram Quasi Agnus
Delas, José Luis de .... Imago
Delden, Lex van.. Fantasia, Op. 87
Diamond, David...................................Elegy in Memory of Maurice Ravel
Dost, Rudolf...La Bal de Béatrice D'Este
Dufourt, Hugues.. Mura Della Citta Di Dite

Compositions Including Keyboard

Balassa, Sándor ....Xenia-Nonet
Barber, Samuel.................................... Medea - Cave of the Heart
Bassett, Leslie ....Nonet
Bauszern, Waldemar von ....Chamber Symphony
Beckwith, John..Circle with Tangents
Bennett, Richard Rodney .... Jazz Calendar
Bentzon, Niels Viggo.......................... Chamber Concerto, Op. 52
Bentzon, Niels Viggo..........Sonata for Twelve Instruments, Op. 257
Benvenuti, Arrigo ....Studi
Berger, Arthur..Chamber Music
Berkeley, Michael.................................Chamber Symphony
Beyer, Frank ....Concertino a Tre
Bianchi, Gabriele................................... Four Studi da Malu
Bland, William.. Sonics I, II, III
Blickhan, Charles Timothy.................... Variations/Permutations
Bloch, Ernest .... Four Episodes
Boesmans, Philippe...Explosives
Bogusławski, Edward.................................... Intonazioni I
Bois, Rob du..Circle
Bolcom, William..Session IV
Borstlap, Dick..Fanfare II
Borstlap, Dick..................................Over de Verandering
Boykan, Martin .... Concerto
Bozay, Attila ....Serie, Op. 19
Bozay, Attila ....Sorozat
Božič, Darijan.................... Concerto Grosso in F Major
Bozza, Eugène................Messe Solennelle de Ste. Cécile
Bresgen, Cesar................................ Kammerkonzert, Op. 6
Brown, Earle...Pentathis
Brown, Jonathan Bruce .... Fragments
Brown, Rayner...........................Passacaglia With Fugues
Brün, Herbert................................Gestures for Eleven
Büchtger, Fritz....................................... Concertino II
Caturla, Alejandro.. Bembe
Caturla, Alejandro....................................Tres Danzas Cubanas
Cazden, Norman .... Concerto for Ten Instruments
Cervetti, Sergio.................................Six Sequences for Dance
Chance, Nancy...Darksong
Charbonnier, Janine...Systems
Chemin-Petit, Hans...........................Suite, Dr. Johannes Faust
Childs, Barney....................................... Jack's New Bag
Chou, Wen-Chung ....Two Miniatures from T'Ang
Chou, Wen-Chung .... Yun
Clementi, Aldo ....Concertino in forma di Variazioni
Constant, Marius.................................... Musique de Concert
Copland, Aaron....................................Appalachian Spring Suite
Crosse, Gordon .... Ariadne
Davidovsky, Mario.. Inflexions
Davis, Anthony...Hemispheres
Delas, José Luis de .... Imago
Delden, Lex van...................................... Nonet, Op. 101

Rychlik, Józef ....Africky Cyklus
Samuel, Gerhard................................ Cold When the Drum Sounds for Dawn
Satie, Erik..Messe Des Pauvres
Saxton, Robert ....Reflections of Narziss & Goldmund
Schäffer, Bogusław ....Permutationen
Schiller, Henryk ....Music No. 2
Schuller, Gunther...Atonal Jazz Study
Schuller, Gunther...Atonal Study in Jazz
Schuller, Gunther.. Automation
Schuller, Gunther..Music From Yesterday in Fact
Schuller, Gunther.. Transformation
Schuller, Gunther.. Twelve by Eleven
Schuller, Gunther...................... Variants on a Theme of John Lewis
Schuller, Gunther..............................Variants on a Theme of Thelonious Monk
Schuman, William... Night Journey
Schwantner, Joseph...Diaphonia Intervallum
Sheriff, Noam ....Music
Siqueira, José de Lima ....Pregao for Eleven Instruments
Smalley, Roger ....Missa Parodia II
Soegijo, Paul... To Catch A Fly
Stewart, Robert...Nonet
Stockhausen, Karlheinz .... Kontra-Punkte No. 1
Strandberg, Newton.. Verses for Five
Štuhec, Igor...Ction
Stürmer, Bruno ....Suite
Szymanski, Pawel..Quasi una Sinfonietta
Tanenbaum, Elias...29526 T
Taub, Bruce ....Chamber Variations 4
Tremblay, George...Champs II (Souffles)
Tremblay, George...Sérénade
Trimble, Lester...Panels I
Trombly, Preston...Chamber Concerto
Urbanner, Erich... Lyrica
Van der Velden, Renier...Etude
Vlad, Roman.. Serenata
Vogt, Hans...Concertino
Volans, Kevin.. Chevron
Vriend, Jan ....Paroesie
Vries, Klaas de .... Moeilijkheden
Webern, Anton von..Concerto, Op. 24
Werle, Lars Johan ....Summer Music
Wilder, Alec..A Debutante's Diary
Wilson, George.. Concatenations
Wiszniewski, Zbigniew.................................. Chamber Music No. 4
Wolf-Ferrari, Ermanno ....Kammersymphonie, Op. 8
Wolff, Christian...Nine
Wuorinen, Charles...Canzona
Wuorinen, Charles...Chamber Concerto
Wuorinen, Charles..The Winds
Yttrehus, Rolv .... Music for Winds, Percussion & Viola
Zillig, Winfried ....Serenade No. 4

Zonn, Paul .... Canzonni, Overo Sonate Concertare Con-Serere

Compositions Including Saxophone

Albright, William .... Marginal Worlds
Andriessen, Jurriaan... Hommage à Milhaud
Bennett, Richard Rodney.. Jazz Calendar
Bentzon, Niels Viggo..Climate Changes, Op. 474
Bois, Rob du..Circle
Borstlap, Dick..Fanfare II
Borstlap, Dick...Over de Verandering
Božič, Darijan... Concerto Grosso in F Major
Bumcke, Gustav...Promenades, Op. 22
Constant, Marius..Musique de Concert
Cunningham, Michael..Spring Sonnet
Custer, Arthur..Cycle for Nine Instruments
DuBois, Robert .... Espace à Remplir Pour Onze Musiciens
Eller, Heino .... Camera Eye
Fortner, Jack...Spring
Gibson, Jon Charles .... Melody IV
Glass, Philip..Glassworks
Grandert, Johann..Nonett
Harbison, John ....Confinement
Hartley, Walter... Double Concerto
Heider, Werner..Sonatina
Hespos, Hans-Joachim ....Break
Hespos, Hans-Joachim ....Keime und Male
Hespos, Hans-Joachim ....Passagen
Holloway, Robin .... Concertino No. 3
Jenni, Donald ....Allegro
Legrand, Michel ....Porcelaine de Saxe
Lewis, Anthony... Pieces of Eight
Lewis, John..Milanese Story
Lybbert, Donald ....Sonorities
Matsushita, Shin-Ichi..Correlations for 3 Groups
Mingus, Charles..Revelations
Nilsson, Bo .... Zeitpunkte
Nono, Luigi..Canti per 13
Paumgartner, Bernhard ....Divertimento
Reck, David ....Number 1 for 12 Performers
Saxton, Robert ....Reflections of Narziss & Goldmund
Schäffer, Bogusław ....Permutationen
Schuller, Gunther..Abstraction
Schuller, Gunther...Atonal Jazz Study
Schuller, Gunther...Atonal Study in Jazz
Schuller, Gunther.. Automation
Schuller, Gunther.....................................Music From Yesterday in Fact

Schuller, Gunther... Transformation
Schuller, Gunther... Twelve by Eleven
Schuller, Gunther.................................... Variants on a Theme of John Lewis
Schuller, Gunther....................Variants on a Theme of Thelonious Monk
Schwantner, Joseph...Diaphonia Intervallum
Schwertsik, Kurt .... Salotto Romano, Op. 5
Tanenbaum, Elias...29526 T
Tanenbaum, Elias... Trios I, II, III
Tarenskeen, Boudewijn .... Machtelt Suite
Vries, Klaas de .... Moeilijkheden
Wilder, Alec..A Debutante's Diary

Compositions Including Percussion

Abrahamsen, Hans..Lied in Fall
Abrahamsen, Hans..Märchenbilder
Adler, Samuel...Concert Piece
Adler, Samuel.. Music for Eleven
Adler, Samuel...Praeludium
Albright, William .... Marginal Worlds
Alpaerts, Flor...Treurdicht
Alsina, Carlos ....Auftrag
Alsina, Carlos ....Funktionen, Op. 14
Alwyn, William...Fanfare for a Joyful Occasion
Andriessen, Jurriaan..Antifona e Fusione
Andriessen, Jurriaan.. Entrata Festiva
Andriessen, Jurriaan..Rouw Past Elektra...
Antheil, George... Ballet Mechanique
Antoniou, Théodore .... Concertino, Op. 21
Antunes, Jorge...Intervertige
Aubin, Tony..Cressida Fanfare
Bäck, Sven-Erik..Chamber Symphony
Baervoets, Raymond ....Fanfare Héroique & Fanfare Joyeuse
Balassa, Sándor ....Xenia-Nonet
Barber, Samuel...Mutations from Bach
Beach, Bruce ....Five Intagli
Beadell, Robert..Introduction and Allegro
Beale, James .... Five Still Lifes, Op. 32
Becker, Gunther...Game for Nine
Beckhelm, Paul... Tragic March
Benhamou, Maurice..Mizmor-Chir
Bennett, Richard Rodney... Jazz Calendar
Bentzon, Niels Viggo................................Chamber Concerto, Op. 52
Bentzon, Niels Viggo.......................................Climate Changes, Op. 474
Bentzon, Niels Viggo........................ Sinfonia Concertante, Op. 100
Benvenuti, Arrigo ....Studi
Beyer, Howard..Suite for Brass Instruments

Jolivet, André...Fanfares pour Britannicus
Jongen, Joseph.................................... Fanfare Héroique, Op. 110
Kahowez, Günter ....Bardo-Puls
Kanitz, Ernest ....Serenade
Kapr, Jan... Omaggio Alla Tromba
Kee, Cornelis...Blijde Incomste
Ketting, Otto .... Intrada Festiva
Ketting, Otto .... Variazioni per Orchestra
Killmayer, Wilhelm ....Kindertage
Knox, Charles.. Symphony
Knox, Charles....................................Symphony for Brass & Percussion
Kocscár, Miklós..Capricorn Concerto
Koellreuter, Hans Joachim ....Constructio ad Synesin 1962
Kohn, Karl... The Prophet Bird
Kolb, Barbara .... Trobar Clus
Kopelent, Marek..............................A Few Minutes with an Oboist
Krenek, Ernst....................................Drei Lustige Märsche, Op. 44
Krenek, Ernst.. Marginal Sounds
Kroeger, Karl..................... The Firebugs Overture and Incidental Music
Kubik, Gail...Divertimento No. 1
Kupferman, Meyer...Infinites 14
Kurka, Robert............................ The Good Soldier Schweik Polka and Waltz
Lanza, Alcides...Eidesis II - 1967 - III
Lebič, Lojze ....Kons (A)
Lebič, Lojze .... Kons (b)
Lebow, Leonard ....Suite for Brass
Lees, Benjamin...Fanfare for a Centennial
Legrand, Michel ....Porcelaine de Saxe
Lehmann, Hans..Quanti
Leleu, Jeanne..Suite Symphonique
Lewis, Anthony.. Pieces of Eight
Lewis, John..Milanese Story
Lewis, Robert .... Music for Twelve Players
Liadov, Anatoli...Fanfares
Lieberson, Peter ....Lalita - Chamber Variations
Ligeti, György...Fragment
Lombardi, Luca..Gespräch über Bäume
Louel, Jean...Fanfare J.M.
Louel, Jean...Fanfares
Luening, Otto .... Fanfare for a Festive Occasion
Lutoslawski, Witold... Slides
Maderna, Bruno ....Serenata No. 2
Maes, Jef ....De Verloofden
Manzoni, Giacomo..Parafrasi Con Finale
Maros, Rudolf.. Musica da Camera
Mason, Benedict............ Imposing a Regular Pattern in Chaos and Heterophony
Mason, Benedict.. The Hinterstoisser Traverse
Matsudaira, Yoritsune.. Serenata
Matsushita, Shin-Ichi.............................Correlations for 3 Groups
Matthews, Colin ....Ceres
Matthews, William...Letters from Home

Powell, Mel.. Modules
Presser, William... Passacaglia and Fugue
Ramovš, Primož..Enneaphonia
Rasmussen, Karl Aage..................................... Movements on a Moving Line
Reck, David .... Number 1 for 12 Performers
Revueltas, Silvestre ....Homenaje a Federico García Lorca
Revueltas, Silvestre .... Ocho por Radio
Revueltas, Silvestre .... Three Sonnets
Reynolds, Roger .... Quick Are the Mouths of Earth
Reynolds, Roger .... The Promises of Darkness
Reynolds, Roger .... Wedge
Reynolds, Verne ....Prelude and Allegro
Reynolds, Verne ....Theme and Variations
Ricci-Signorini, Antonio ....Fantasia Burlesca in C Major
Rosseau, Norbert...Fanfare, Op. 58
Rovics, Howard.. Events II
Rovsing   Olsen, Poul.....................................Patet per Nove Musici, Op. 55
Rowland, David.. Tropisms
Ruders, Poul ....4 Dances in 1 Movement
Ruders, Poul .... Nightshade
Rudziński, Zbigniew...Sonata
Ruyneman, Daniel ....Hieroglyphs
Rydman, Kari... Khoros No. 1
Saint-Saëns, Camille.................................... Le Carnaval Des Animaux
Santoro, Claudio ....Intermitencias II
Satie, Erik..Messe Des Pauvres
Schäfer, Karl...Spielmusik
Schäffer, Bogusław ....Permutationen
Schifrin, Lalo.. Ritual of Sound
Schiller, Henryk ....Music No. 2
Schmitt, Franz.............................Fanfare, Le Camp de Pompée, Op. 69
Schmitt, Franz...Tullnerbacher Blasmusik
Schönherr, Max ....Dance
Schuller, Gunther...Abstraction
Schuller, Gunther.......................................Atonal Jazz Study
Schuller, Gunther.......................................Atonal Study in Jazz
Schuller, Gunther... Automation
Schuller, Gunther...........................Music From Yesterday in Fact
Schuller, Gunther.................................Progression in Tempo
Schuller, Gunther....................................... Transformation
Schuller, Gunther....................................... Twelve by Eleven
Schuller, Gunther............................ Variants on a Theme of John Lewis
Schuller, Gunther...............Variants on a Theme of Thelonious Monk
Schumann, Georg ....Suite für Blechbläser und Pauken
Schwartz, Elliott.................................Concert Piece for Ten Players
Schwertsik, Kurt .... Salotto Romano, Op. 5
Shahan, Paul..Leipzig Towers
Shahan, Paul..Spectrums
Silverman, Stanley ....Planh
Skalkottas, Nikos...................................Andante Sostenuto
Sollberger, Harvey................................. Chamber Variations

Title Index

Auftrag... Carlos Alsina
Automation ....Gunther Schuller
Bagatelles, Op. 35...Ben Frankel
La Bal de Béatrice D'Este.......................................Rudolf Dost
La Bal de Béatrice D'Este.................................. Reynaldo Hahn
Baletti a 9 .... Jan Novák
Ballet Méchanique...George Antheil
Baltic Sonnets.......................................Ryszard Kwiatkowski
Bardo-Puls.. Günter Kahowez
Basses and Brass... Bruno Amato
Battaglia...Thomas Bucchi
Bembe ....Alejandro Caturla
Bits .... George Edwards
Bläsermusik, Op. 43 ....Werner Thärichen
Blijde Incomste...Cornelis Kee
3 Brass Cats ....Chris Hazell
The Brass Square..Earl Zindars
Brassy Prelude, Op. 31, No. 1....................................Rudolf Ganz
Bravura Prelude..................................... George Frederick McKay
Break.. Hans-Joachim Hespos
Bridges II.. Yuji Takahashi
Brighton Piece...Anthony Gilbert
Byzantine Suite .... Carl Hugo Grimm
Cadence.. Ezra Laderman
Cadenze.. Siegfried Naumann
Camera Eye .... Heino Eller
Canti per 13...Luigi Nono
Canticle...William Francis McBeth
Canzona...Charles Wuorinen
Canzona Moderna in Homage to G. Gabrieli ....David Uber
Three Canzonas..Gordon Binkerd
Canzonni, Overo Sonate Concertare Con-Serere .... Paul Zonn
Cañon (Canyon)... Thom Hutcheson
Capriccio ....Jacques Ibert
Capriccio... Krzysztof Penderecki
Capricorn Concerto..Miklós Kocscár
Caractères.. Antoine Tisne
Le Carnaval Des Animaux ....Camille Saint-Saëns
Cassation, Hob. II:C3.....................................Franz Joseph Haydn
Cassazione, K. 63.............................Wolfgang Amadeus Mozart
Cassazione, K. 99.............................Wolfgang Amadeus Mozart
Cassazione, No. 2 in G Major, Hob. II:G1 ....Franz Joseph Haydn
Cassazione, No. 3 in G Major, Hob. II:9.........................Franz Joseph Haydn
Catalisis.. Jorge Cervelló
To Catch A Fly ....Paul Soegijo
Cathedral Music...Samuel Thomas Beversdorf
Caucasian Sketches, Dans la Mosque......................Mikhail Ippolitov-Ivanov
Ceremonial and Flourish.................................... Richard Arnell
Ceremonial and Flourish, Op. 43 ....Richard Arnell
Ceremonial Fanfare..Aaron Copland
Ceremonial Fanfare...Walter Piston

Divertimento for Slavko Osterc .... Ivo Petrić
Divertimento I, Op. 79 .... Jan Zdeněk Bartoš
Divertimento in Bb Major .... Anton Liber
Divertimento in D Major .... Franz Joseph Haydn
Divertimento No. 1 .... Gail Kubik
Divertimento No. 2 .... Oscar van Hemel
Divertimento, K. 113 .... Wolfgang Amadeus Mozart
Divertimento, K. 131 .... Wolfgang Amadeus Mozart
Divertimento, K. 166 .... Wolfgang Amadeus Mozart
Divertimento, K. 186 .... Wolfgang Amadeus Mozart
Divertimento, K. 187 .... Wolfgang Amadeus Mozart
Divertimento, K. 188 .... Wolfgang Amadeus Mozart
Divertimento, Op. 49 .... Karl Schiske
Divertimento, Op. 53 .... Fritz Leitermeyer
Divertissement .... Jean Emile Bernard
Divertissement .... Werner Egk
Divertissement .... Pierre Hasquenoph
Divertissement .... Lode Huybrechts
Divertissement .... Albert Perilhou
Divertissement .... Lynden de Young
Divertissement and Musette .... Gustave Samazeuilh
Divertissement In D Major, Hob. II:8 .... Franz Joseph Haydn
Divertissement No. 2 in F Major .... Franz Joseph Haydn
Divertissement Nocturne .... Jean-Marie Depelsenaire
Divertissement pour Dixtuor .... Pierre Hasquenoph
Divertissement, Op. 36 .... Jean Emile Bernard
Divertissement, Op. 40 .... Raymond Chevreville
Divisions .... Jürg Wyttenbach
Dixtuor .... Claude Arrieu
Dixtuor .... Théodore Dubois
Dixtuor .... Georges Enesco
Dixtuor .... Henri C. Van Praag
Dixtuor à cordes .... Darius Milhaud
Dixtuor in F Minor .... Ange Flegier
Dixtuor, Op. 103 .... Emanuel Moór
Dorfmusikanten Op. 14 .... Cesar Bresgen
The Dorian Horizon, Echores .... Toru Takemitsu
Dos Poemas, Op. 10, No. 16 & 42 .... Jacobo Ficher
Double Concerto .... Walter Hartley
Double Quintet .... Robert Saxton
Double Quintet .... Gunther Schuller
Double Wind Quintet .... Alfred Reed
Double Woodwind Quintet .... David Jaeger
Dramata .... Václav Kučera
Dumbarton Oaks Concerto .... Igor Stravinsky
Twelve Ecossaises .... Jan E. Doležálek
Eidesis II - 1967 - III .... Alcides Lanza
El-Greco-Fantasie .... Gladys Nordenstrom
Elegy in Memory of K. Rathaus .... Paul Turok
Elegy in Memory of Maurice Ravel .... David Diamond
11 Instruments .... Morton Feldman

Fanfare, Op. 58..Norbert Rosseau
Fanfares...Anatoli Liadov
Fanfares...Jean Louel
Fanfares...Raymond Moulaert
Two Fanfares...George Heussenstam
Two Fanfares, Op. 49...Martin Mailman
Fanfares and Processional..Anthony Payne
Fanfares Liturgiques...Henri-Frédien Tomasi
Fanfares pour Britannicus...André Jolivet
Fanfares pour Tous les Temps ....André-Charles Ameller
Fant'sy II... Evans Williams
Fantasia...William Ward
Fantasia Burlesca in C Major........................... Antonio Ricci-Signorini
Fantasia Concertante per 12...................................Virgilio Mortari
Fantasia No. 2 .... Armando Gentilucci
Fantasia, Op. 87 ....Lex van Delden
Fantasie.. Henri C. Van Praag
Fantasy for Nine Wind Instruments ....Eugene Goossens
Fasce Sonore (6+5) .... Riccardo Nielsen
Feldpartitur, Chorale St. Antoine, Hob. II:46.....................Franz Joseph Haydn
Festival Fanfare...William Havergal Brian
Festliche Fanfare ....Wolfgang Steffen
A Few Minutes with an Oboist...Marek Kopelent
The Firebugs Overture and Incidental Music ....Karl Kroeger
Fischerhaus-Serenade, Op. 45 ....Hans Erich Apostel
5 Concertante Epigram-Schetsen, Op. 159..............................Gerard Boedijn
5 Invocaciones al Crucificado......................... Bassols Xavier Montsalvatge
5 Tempos for 11 Instruments ....Shin-Ichi Matsushita
Fluxus, Op. 7...Girolamo Arrigo
Folia...Charles Dodge
Folkloristische Suite .... Adriaan Bonsel
4 Compositions.. Poul Ruders
4 Dances in 1 Movement... Poul Ruders
4 Scenes for 10, Op. 21, No. 1 ....Horst Ebenhoh
Fragment.. Juan Guinjoàn
Fragment...György Ligeti
Fragments .... Jonathan Bruce Brown
Frequenzen... Bo Nilsson
Fuga No. 4 ....Ernest Mulder
Fugerat Forspel... Bjorn Schildknecht
Fugue in D Minor.. Donald Haddad
Funktionen, Op. 14.. Carlos Alsina
Galimathias Musicum, K. 32 ....Wolfgang Amadeus Mozart
Game for Nine.. Gunther Becker
Gathering ....David Olan
Geduldspiel...Hans Abrahamsen
Genesis, Op. 19, No. 2..Henryk Mikolaj Górecki
Gespräch über Bäume..Luca Lombardi
Gestures for Eleven...Herbert Brün
Glassworks...Philip Glass
Gloria in Excelsis ....David Uber

Bibliography

Arnold, Denis. "Chamber Music." *The New Oxford Companion to Music*. Ed. Arnold. Oxford: Oxford University Press, 1983. Vol. 1. 343-8.

_____. "Concerto." *The New Oxford Companion*. Vol. 1. 463.

Birdle, Reginald Smith. *Contemporary Percussion*. London: Oxford University Press, 1970.

Blades, James. *Percussion Instruments and Their History*. New York: Frederick A. Praeger, Pub., 1970.

Bradshaw, Susan. "Whatever Happened to Chamber Music?" *Tempo* 123 (Dec. 1977) 7-9.

Brook, Barry S. "Symphonie Concertante." *The New Grove Dictionary of Music and Musicians*. Ed. Sadie. London: Macmillian Pub. Ltd., 1980. Vol. 18. 425.

_____. "The Symphonie Concertante: An Interim Report." *The Musical Quarterly* 47, (1961): 493-505.

Camus, Raoul. "Bands." *The New Grove Dictionary of American Music*. Ed. Hitchcock and Sadie. London: Macmillian Pub. Ltd., 1986. Vol. I. 127-37.

Carse, Adam. *The Orchestra in the XVIII Century*. New York: Broude Brothers Limited, 1969.

Cope, David. *New Directions in Music*. 4th ed. Dubuque, Iowa: Wm. C. Brown Pub., 1984.

Craft, Robert. "Performance Notes for Schoenberg's Quintet." *Woodwind Magazine* (June, 1952): 6-7+.

Cross, Milton and Ewen, David. "Richard Strauss." *New Encyclopedia of the Great Composers and Their Music* . Garden City, N.Y.: Doubleday & Company, Inc., 1969. Vol. 2. 970-71.

Earls, Paul and Richard Kassel. "Partch, Harry." *The New Grove Dictionary of American Music*. Vol 3. 481-83.

Goldman, Richard Franko. "American Music: 1918-1960." *The New Oxford History of Music*. Ed. Cooper. London: Oxford University Press, 1974. Vol. X. 569-634.

Griffiths, Paul. "Chamber Music: The 20th Century." *The New Oxford Companion*. Vol. 1. 348-349.

Malm, William P. *Music Cultures of the Pacific, the Near East, and Asia*. Englewood Cliffs, N.J.: Prentice-Hall, 1967.

Meyer, Eve R. "The Viennese Divertimento." *The Music Review* 29 (1968): 165-171.

Morgan, Robert P. *Twentieth-Century Music*. New York: W.W. Norton & Co., 1991.

Mostel, R. "Chamber Orchestra Sounds Like Chamber Music (26-member Ensemble Eschews a Conductor)." *Chamber Music Magazine* 6 (1989): 20-21+.

Murray, Sterling E., ed. "Five Wind Partitias," by Antonio Rosetti. *Recent Researches in the Music of the Classical Era* . Madison: A-R Editions, Inc., 1989. Vols. 30-31. viii-iv.

The New Harvard Dictionary of Music, 1986 ed. S.v. "Chamber Music." Vol. 1. 146-7.

The New Oxford Companion to Music, 1983 ed. S.v. "Cassation.". Vol. 1. 321.

The New Oxford Companion to Music, 1983 ed. S.v. "Serenade." Vol. 2. 1667-8.

Peyser, Joan, ed. *The Orchestra: Origins and Transformations*. New York: Charles Scribner's Sons, 1986.

Pleyel, Ignaz. "Periodical Symphonies." Ed. Raymond R. Smith. *Recent Researches in Music of the Classical Era* . Vol. 8. Madison, Wis.: A-R Editions, Inc., 1978.

Rowen, Ruth Halle. *Early Chamber Music*. New York: Columbia University Press, 1949; reprint, New York: Da Capo Press, 1974.

Simms, Bryan R. "Twentieth-Century Composers Return to the Small Ensemble." Peyser, ed. *The Orchestra*. 455-478.

Sirmen, Maddalena Laura Lombardini. "Violin Concertos." Ed. Jane L. Berdes. *Recent Researches in Music of the Classical Era* . Vol. 38. Madison, Wis.: A-R Edition, Inc., 1991

Smith, Erik. *Mozart Serenades, Divertimenti and Dances*. London: BBC, 1982.

Stolba, K. Marie. *The Development of Western Music: A History*. Dubuque: Wm. C. Brown Pub., 1990.

Swed, Mark. "Back to the Future: The Return of the Composer's Ensemble." *Chamber Music* 5 (1988): 14-17.

Thompson, Wendy. "Divertimento." *The New Oxford Companion*. Vol. 1. 561.

_____. "Sinfonia Concertante." *The New Oxford Companion*. Vol. 2. 1778-9.

Ulrich, Homer. *Chamber Music*. 2nd ed. New York: Columbia University Press, 1966.

Unverricht, Hubert. "Cassation." *The New Grove*. Vol. 3. 859-60.

_____. "Divertimento." *The New Grove*. Vol. 5. 504-6.

_____. "Notturno." *The New Grove*. Vol. 13. 431.

_____. "Serenade." *The New Grove*. Vol. 17. 159-60.

Walsh, Stephen. "Davies, Peter Maxwell." *The New Grove*. Vol. 5. 276.

Webster, James. "Towards a History of Viennese Chamber Music in the Early Classical Period." *Journal of the American Musicological Society* 27 (1974): 212-247.

Westrup, Jack . *Schubert Chamber Music* . Seattle: University of Washington Press, 1969.

White, Eric Walter. *Stravinsky: The Composer and His Works*. Berkeley and Los Angeles: University of California Press, 1972.